Buses and Coaches 1945–70
From Contemporary Adverts

GAVIN BOOTH

BRITAIN'S BUSES SERIES, VOLUME 13

Front cover image: The front page of the monthly trade magazines was a sought-after spot. Park Royal-Roe, part of the ACV Group, ran a series of adverts using an artist's impression of a recent delivery against an appropriate townscape. This image appeared on the front cover of the January 1965 *Bus & Coach* magazine and features a 1964 Manchester Corporation Leyland Panther with Park Royal bodywork.

Title page image: This detail is from a 1954 Crossley advert, featuring an artistic impression of an anonymous municipal Regent V with Crossley bodywork. Although Crossley had been acquired by AEC in 1948 to create, with Maudslay, the ACV Group, AEC badged some of its products as Crossleys, often to qualify for extra space at the Commercial Motor Show.

Contents page image: Bus and coach manufacturers commissioned artists to create dramatic images to help sell their products. This detail from a 1956 ACV advert shows an anonymous AEC Reliance coach with a Roe Dalesman body – built by another company in the ACV Group – apparently en route to London. This illustration is much more realistic than many others that exaggerated the length and streamlining of coach bodies; some are included in this book.

Published by Key Books
An imprint of Key Publishing Ltd
PO Box 100
Stamford
Lincs PE19 1XQ

www.keypublishing.com

The right of Gavin Booth to be identified as the author of this book has been asserted in accordance with the Copyright, Designs and Patents Act 1988 Sections 77 and 78.

Copyright © Gavin Booth, 2022

ISBN 978 1 80282 384 4

All rights reserved. Reproduction in whole or in part in any form whatsoever or by any means is strictly prohibited without the prior permission of the Publisher.

Typeset by SJmagic DESIGN SERVICES, India.

Contents

Chapter 1   Reaching Prospective Customers 4
Chapter 2   1945–50: Post-war Austerity 10
Chapter 3   1951–55: The Underfloor Revolution 28
Chapter 4   1956–60: Double-Deck Developments 46
Chapter 5   1961–65: Single-Deck Developments 62
Chapter 6   1966–70: Moving to Standardisation 80

Chapter 1
Reaching Prospective Customers

For the bus and coach trade press in the early post-war years, advertising revenue was buoyant, as suppliers vied to catch the attention of senior managers looking for everything from nuts and bolts to brand-new buses and coaches. Several of the new entrants to the coachbuilding market placed simple half-page black-and-white adverts that typically contained a flattering photograph of a recent delivery, plus a few words of text and the company's name in bold with an address and phone number underneath.

Some of the more ambitious newcomers splashed out on full-page adverts, and, if they were feeling particularly confident, they might opt for a second colour or even a full-colour advert. The second colour took away from the uniformity of the monochrome and helped adverts to stand out, but the only trouble could be what the second colour was, particularly if advertisers found themselves with a second colour that was inappropriate for the true livery of the bus or coach featured. Many of the new entrants competing for orders for coach bodywork from smaller operators that emerged in the 1940s, had gone by the mid-1950s.

Effective full-colour adverts using photographs were still to come, as design studios, advertisers, block-makers, and printers worked to produce an acceptable result. Artists were kept busy, producing dramatic

A reminder of the varied bus and coach advertising in the 1930s. This TSM (formerly Tilling-Stevens) 1931 advert uses colour to portray a TSM Express supplied to Portsmouth Corporation. Colour illustrations of this type were effective but rare in the days before good four-colour photo reproduction was possible.

and flattering images that sometimes grossly exaggerated the look or the length of the bus or coach featured. As we shall see, the advent of well-reproduced colour photography in the 1950s did not signal the end of unrealistic images, even in the 1960s.

In this introduction, we have included some examples of 1930s trade press advertising, which shows that some advertisers stuck to very conventional designs, while others grasped the opportunity to embrace current design fashions in an attempt to capture the attention of readers faced with dozens of pages of largely black-and-white images.

Through the period covered by this book, it was inevitably the major players that spent most on trade adverts to keep their names in front of potential customers and, of course, their competitors. We shall probably never know how much this expensive advertising resulted in orders being placed by hardheaded bus and coach managers, and how much was to irritate their competitors, but the continued existence of the trade magazines depended greatly on advertising revenue.

But looking through copies of the trade press magazines published between 1945 and 1950, often in the pages of the monthly *Bus & Coach*, it is interesting to note that some manufacturers spent little or nothing on advertising. So, while Duple, market leader as a builder of coach bodies, rarely missed an issue with full-page, often full-colour adverts, the companies that would increasingly challenge Duple in the 1950s – Burlingham, Harrington and Plaxtons – booked few adverts in the 1940s, yet their businesses continued to grow.

The trade magazines issued to coincide with the biennial Commercial Motor Show tended to carry the most adverts, often encouraging readers to visit their stands at the shows. The 1948 show was the first since the 1930s, so there was a great effort to impress visitors with brand-new buses and coaches, many of them British-built for export customers. The October 1948 issue of *Bus & Coach,* published to coincide with the opening of the Commercial Motor Transport Exhibition at Earl's Court, included 104 pages of advertising placed by 143 suppliers, contrasting with just 40 pages of editorial; the October 1952 issue of the same magazine, in advance of that year's show, had 132 pages of advertising placed by 159 suppliers, supporting 46 editorial pages.

Using just black, Maudslay catches the eye with this 1936 angled advert, promoting its advanced SF40 model, which offered 40 seats and an entrance ahead of the front axle.

If manufacturers wanted to make a splash, often at Commercial Motor Show time with an important new model to reveal, they took double-page spreads in the trade magazines, and sometimes stretched even to three-page as well as fold-out adverts. These did not come cheap but were seen as the best way to keep your name and products in the limelight.

Some advertisers made outrageous claims about their products – remember these mainly appeared before the 1968 Trade Description Act. In this book, you will find headlines like 'World famed for craftsmanship and design'; 'The rear engine has put the forward engine behind for all time' (this in a 1952 advert); 'Design – brilliant, construction – superb!'; and 'Proven the world's most practical bus chassis'.

And the structure of the manufacturing industry was changing. As early as 1948, there were acquisitions and mergers that streamlined the shape of the industry. AEC and Leyland, with the capacity to build the most bus chassis, supported the trade magazines with regular adverts. When Associated Commercial Vehicles (ACV) was set up in 1948, ultimately bringing together chassis manufacturers AEC, Crossley and Maudslay, and bodybuilders Crossley, Park Royal and Roe, there were already signs of a rationalised approach to advertising, so while all of these companies once placed individual adverts, under ACV it turned out that only AEC and Park Royal-Roe

Above left: General Motors was still promoting the German-built Opel in the British trade press in 1939, just months before the outbreak of war.

Above right: Sentinel had displayed the first commercially available underfloor-engined bus in 1948, and at the 1950 Commercial Show it was claiming that this Ribble STC6 was the highlight of the show. If Ribble's intention was to rattle its near-neighbour Leyland into action with its own underfloor-engined chassis, it worked. After 1951, Ribble bought no more Sentinels and returned to Leyland models in a big way. Although few Sentinel buses were sold, the company was a regular advertiser in the trade press.

would advertise, with the consequent reduction in potential advertising revenue for the trade press publishers.

AEC's adverts were more varied, often in different styles and featuring new models. Park Royal-Roe advertising was more predictable for a number of years, with a formulaic series of black-and-white adverts, each featuring a recent delivery; unsurprisingly, perhaps, many featured Park Royal and Roe bodies on AEC chassis. Later, as we shall see, Park Royal-Roe opted for full-colour adverts, often booking the prestigious front-cover slot.

Leyland ploughed a different furrow. Its advertising copy was often peppered with facts, figures and percentages, and while it was building bodies on its own chassis until 1954, it was no great surprise that the buses featured usually carried Leyland bodies.

Of the other major chassis builders, Bristol continued to advertise until 1949, by which time its products, and those of its sister company Eastern Coach Works (ECW) were only available to the captive market of state-owned operators, removing the need to advertise. After Bristol chassis became generally available again, from 1965, it became a regular advertiser once more.

Daimler advertising often homed in on technical features of its chassis, and rarely featured its bread-and-butter products, double-deck chassis. This may have been because these tended to sell themselves, and when complete vehicles were featured, they were examples of Daimler's underfloor-engined single-deck Freeline chassis, which did not always perform as well as hoped in the home market.

Above left: Bus industry suppliers sometimes featured buses in their advertising, like this 1948 coloured black-and-white photo of a London Transport AEC Regent STL type entering Trafalgar Square with the Lodge Plugs name prominent.

Above right: Guy's famous Indian's Head radiator filler cap and prominent 'GUY' lettering was used to dramatic effect in this 1949 advert, underlining the Guy slogan 'Feathers in our cap'. Guy was based in Wolverhampton.

For many years, Guy booked the inside front cover spot in *Bus & Coach* magazine, for a series of black-and-white adverts that included a disappointingly small image of a recent delivery, or veered to the other extreme with dramatic adverts featuring the Guy name and Indian's Head filler cap.

Dennis was a regular advertiser, often featuring coaches built on its Lancet chassis, but as orders dwindled, so did its advertising budget. Dennis, of course, lives on to be the one British chassis builder from the 1940s that has survived into the 2020s.

The builders of bus and coach bodies were less consistent in their approach to advertising. As we have seen, Duple had the luxury coach market sewn up for many years. Unlike the builders of service bus bodies that were looking for decent-sized orders from the larger municipal, company and independent fleets – and of course London Transport – Duple was also promoting its wares to the smaller independents that came back year after year for a few new coaches to start each summer season. And so, most Duple adverts featured its coach bodies mounted on lightweight chassis, typically Bedford and Commer, and later Ford.

Looking back, it is notable how few adverts were placed in the 1940s and 1950s by Duple's main competitors, Burlingham, Harrington and Plaxtons, which were based in the English seaside towns of Blackpool, Hove and Scarborough, respectively. Although their products were growing in popularity in the 1950s, they rarely advertised them. This does not seem to have harmed them, as they had a steady stream of bodies coming out of their coachworks.

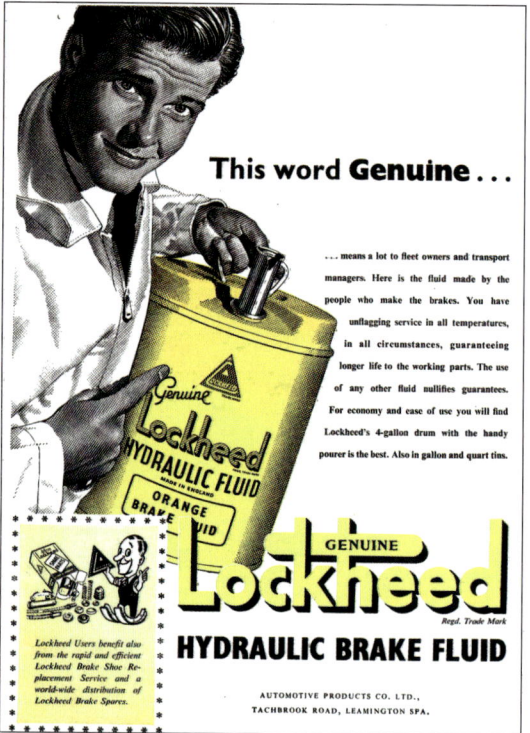 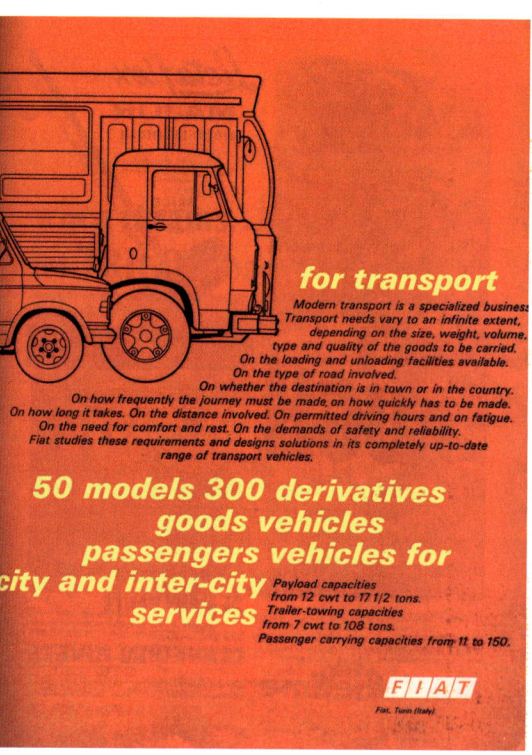

Above left: Roger Moore was destined to become an internationally famous film star, but, in 1952, as a struggling actor, he was earning extra money as a model, and is seen here advertising Lockheed hydraulic brake fluid.

Above right: Before buses and coaches built in mainland Europe became familiar in Britain, Fiat was dipping a tentative toe in the British market with this advert, from the February 1970 final issue of *Bus & Coach*. As Iveco, Fiat buses and coaches were imported, but less successfully than giants like Mercedes-Benz, Scania and Volvo.

Harrington blossomed in the 1960s with its much-admired Cavalier and Grenadier body styles, and although Duple bought Burlingham and later moved its main coachworks from London to Blackpool, Plaxtons really came into its own with the big-windowed Panorama range from 1958, and ultimately grew to acquire Duple and fought through the uncertainties of the 1990s and 2000s to survive as a major force in the British bus industry as an important part of Alexander Dennis.

The leaders in the service bus bodywork market were Park Royal, already mentioned, and MCW, often in direct competition with each other for London and other major body contracts. Firms like Alexander, Northern Counties and Willowbrook lacked the capacity but picked up some useful orders from regular, often local, customers.

MCW's adverts were more varied in content and style than rivals Park Royal-Roe, and, from time to time, diverted from featuring buses built for British operators to highlight export successes as well as its own coach bodies. Its coach bodies never sold in great numbers, probably because operators regarded MCW as purely a builder of service bus bodies.

In the 1940s and 1950s, it would have been unthinkable that, more than half-a-century later, none of these bus builders – AEC, Bedford, Bristol, Daimler, Duple, Guy, Harrington, Leyland, MCW, Park Royal-Roe or Willowbrook – would still be active, and that most UK-built buses would be produced by what were the previously separate business of Alexander, Dennis and Plaxton, now together as Alexander Dennis, as well as two newcomers, Optare and Wrights.

A look back at the post-war bus and coach advertising at its post-war height reveals that in the October 1952 issue of *Bus & Coach* there were 12 adverts for chassis builders and 19 for body builders. Fast forward to the October 1969 issue, following closures, mergers and acquisitions, and the equivalent figures were five and four.

The very last issue of *Bus & Coach* was published just four months later, in February 1970. The writing was on the wall as the number of editorial and advertising pages gradually reduced. In that last issue the only manufacturer adverts were placed by Bristol, Leyland and, interestingly, Fiat – a taste perhaps of the increasing number of manufacturers from mainland Europe that had British business in their sights.

Fast forward more than a decade from 1970, and in its early-1980s advertising, Scania reminded potential customers that there was no such thing as a 100 per cent British bus, underlining that sales of its Swedish-built models were supporting British industry. The bus is a 1982 East Lancs-bodied Scania BR112DH.

Chapter 2
1945–50
Post-war Austerity

After six years of war, bus and coach operators that were working to rebuild their businesses faced the added complication that the largest manufacturers were being encouraged by government to build buses for export, to help rebuild the UK economy, and in turn this encouraged a rush of new companies to try their hand at bodybuilding. Most were small businesses, and many barely survived into the 1950s, but they satisfied a hunger for new vehicles, often from smaller bus and coach operators.

While the bigger fleets awaited their turn in the queue for new buses, many operators recognised that rebuilding and rebodying would be a useful stop-gap exercise. They usually had pre-war and wartime chassis that still had life in them and embarked on a programme to refurbish the sounder bodies and commission new bodies to replace wartime utility bodies that had been built using unseasoned timber.

The larger operators often had facilities to carry out rebuilds, which sometimes resulted in virtually new bodies. Older buses emerged looking less utilitarian, with smoother lines, rubber-mounted windows and an internal refurbishment that usually at least involved replacing wooden-slatted utility seats with proper cushioned ones. Where there was no capacity to do this work in-house, a network of smaller coachbuilders carried out refurbishment exercises that prolonged the life of buses until new post-war deliveries arrived. Many pre-war single-deck coach bodies had already disappeared, as their chassis were rebodied as double-deckers during the war.

Such was the initial demand for new buses and coaches in the early post-war years, that some orders were not fulfilled for perhaps four or five years, at a time when passenger demand was reaching new levels. A consequence of this was that many buses lasted well beyond their normal service lives, until new deliveries started to arrive.

At this time, when every new bus or coach was built in the UK, there were inevitably chassis and body builders that dominated the market – AEC, Bedford, Bristol, Daimler, Guy and Leyland – tended to be the most popular chassis manufacturers, and Alexander, Brush, Burlingham, Duple, MCW, Park Royal, Plaxtons and Willowbrook were the main bodybuilders.

While a cottage industry grew up among new entrants to the bodybuilding business, it was more difficult to break into the bus chassis market. Foden and Sentinel, both well-established truck builders, saw an opportunity after the war to dip a toe in the bus market with innovative designs – Foden with a chassis with a rear-mounted engine and Sentinel with a mid-mounted underfloor engine. But the first operator that anticipated the move to underfloor-engined single-deckers had actually been Midland Red, whose in-house builder, BMMO, managed to get 100 of its S6 models on the road in 1946, while the major manufacturers barely had time to catch their breath after the war.

By 1950, new models were in the pipeline from the major builders and with less restrictive length regulations for single-deck buses and coaches, the decade that followed would see significant changes in single-deck design, as well as early indications of the future layout of double-deckers.

Coaches

Bedford and Duple fared very well in the post-war rush for new coaches with the ubiquitous Bedford OB/Duple Vista pairing, which could be found in fleets of all sizes throughout Britain. This Crosville example, featured in a 1950 advert, has the added attraction of curved roof quarter-lights.

Charles Roberts of Wakefield was an established small coachbuilder that returned to the bus scene between 1947 and 1950 with metal-framed bodies like this four-bay design – four windows between the front axle and the rear entrance – for Sheffield Corporation on AEC Regent III chassis in this dramatic 1948 advert.

Tilling-Stevens had been a pioneering bus manufacturer, as this 1947 advert reminds us, and after World War Two it briefly returned to chassis building at Maidstone, surviving only until 1950 when it was acquired by the Rootes Group.

Elegant Coachwork, certainly, but with more than a nod to contemporary Duple designs. This 1948 advert shows a Maudslay Marathon with Whitson coachwork. Maudslay sold out to the new ACV Group the following year, and Whitson survived in the coach body market until the early 1950s. Maudslay was based in Alcester, and Whitson in Middlesex.

Rebuilds and rebodies

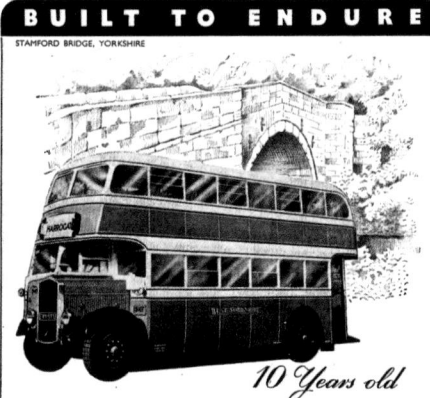

Eastern Coach Works (ECW) at Lowestoft had grown out of the bodybuilding activities of the Eastern Counties bus company and had enjoyed success in the 1930s with its range of bus bodies. This series of 1948 adverts promoted the longevity of its pre-war products. First, the lowbridge 'Long Life' body on a 1938 Crosville Leyland Titan, one of 24 that had each averaged over 500,000 miles and were still regarded as front-line buses ten years later.

The other adverts in this series follow a similar line. The North Western Bristol K5G is one of 12 delivered ten years earlier and in good condition after mileages ranging from 473,000 to 545,000. The life of the bus featured was further extended in 1951 when it received a new Willowbrook body.

The West Yorkshire Bristol K5G is one of 21 delivered in 1937 that had averaged 595,345 miles with one achieving an impressive 665,553 miles.

Opposite: One of the companies that was heavily involved in repairing and rebuilding pre-war buses was Samlesbury Engineering, based near Blackburn. In this 1950 advert, a number of Birmingham City Daimler COG5s are seen undergoing extensive rebuilding to prolong their lives.

Smaller coachbuilders

Many smaller coachbuilders blossomed briefly in the early post-war years, as coach operators rebuilt their businesses. London-based All-Weather took out full-page adverts to promote its Streamline coachwork with stylish period adverts like this 1949 one. The 33-seat coach, on Commer Avenger chassis, has echoes of Duple design – as did many bodies of the time. Commer, part of the Rootes Group, was based in Luton.

Dutfield of Godalming offered 'Craftsmanship in Coachwork plus Comfort & Style'; this 1950 advert features a Tilling-Stevens K6LA7 and a body with strong hints of Duple. Dutfield built its first coach bodies in 1948 and in 1950 joined a co-operative of other builders that survived only into the early 1950s.

Windovers of London built coach bodies from the late 1940s to the mid-1950s and produced some striking designs, although this 1950 advert offers a somewhat exaggerated take on the real thing – a common ploy when artist's impressions were involved. It apparently depicts an AEC Regal IV for Sheffield United Tours.

Opposite: Trans-United Coach-Craft of Rochdale was another co-operative and was connected to the well-known local express coach operator, Yelloway. This 1948 advert claimed to present 'a new high in construction and appointment'. Transun survived into the 1950s, building bodies on the new breed of underfloor-engined chassis. The 33-seater in the advert features a Crossley SD42 chassis.

The major coachbuilders

The long-established Hove-based coachbuilder Harrington specialised in luxury coaches, which for many years featured the distinctive dorsal fin at the rear, a useful means of recognition incorporating an air extractor. This apparently full-fronted coach on Leyland chassis, passing Buckingham Palace, appeared in a 1950 advert. Harrington bodies were popular through to the firm's closure in 1966.

Plaxtons of Scarborough rarely advertised in the trade press at this time, but this 1950 advert features a 'super observation coach' on Leyland Comet chassis, with a Perspex sliding roof and front domes, with toughened glass side domes. The normal control Comet 90 was principally a goods model, but was used for coaches like this one, supplied to operators looking for something larger and more powerful than the Bedford OB.

In the 1940s London-based Duple, for years Britain's leading specialist coach builder, went in for attractive adverts with the minimum of text, featuring paintings by the splendidly named artist Carrington Windo, of anonymous coaches in attractive settings. This slightly exaggerated Leyland Tiger PS1 with Duple A-type bodywork is pictured passing through Thaxted in Essex in this 1948 advert.

Opposite: Carrington Windo again and this 1948 advert features a Vista coach on Bedford OB chassis at Loch Maree. The Bedford OB/Duple Vista was bought by hundreds of operators of all sizes and provided an inexpensive and reliable way to restart coaching after the war. Bedford was based in Dunstable.

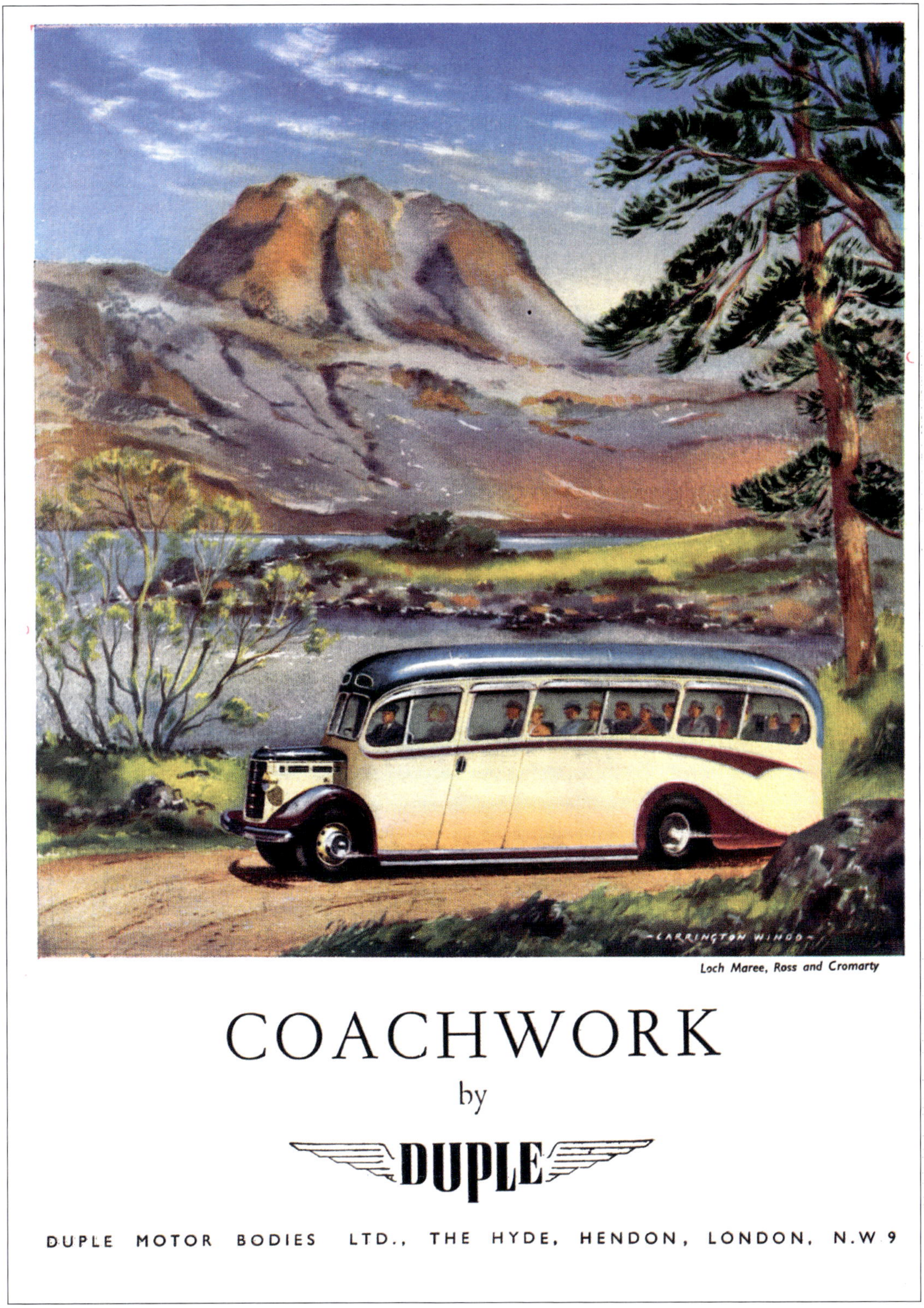

Loch Maree, Ross and Cromarty

COACHWORK
by

DUPLE MOTOR BODIES LTD., THE HYDE, HENDON, LONDON, N.W 9

Export activity

Above: Metropolitan-Cammell-Weymann was one of the major British bodybuilders, and its advert for the 1948 Commercial Motor Traction Exhibition – the first since the 1930s – trumpeted its credentials as a builder of bodywork for operators throughout the world. The home market is represented by a Bristol K6A for Maidstone & District, and the export markets by a Leyland Tiger for Rio de Janeiro, an AEC Regal for Lisbon and an integral BUT trolleybus for Auckland.

Opposite: An advert very much of its time, as Guy Motors of Wolverhampton demonstrated in 1948 that it was following UK government advice and supplying passenger and goods models to Belgium, Ceylon, Holland, Norway, South Africa and Spain. Guy chassis often made up for their lack of refinement with their sturdiness and reliability. The Guy bus range at the time comprised the Arab, Otter, Wolf and Vixen models.

Guy was exporting very British-looking Park Royal-bodied double-deckers to Ceylon in 1948, as featured in this contemporary advert showing a bus delivered to the South Western bus company of Colombo.

In 1949, the Bristol Tramways & Carriage company, based, of course, in Bristol, became part of the state-owned British Transport Commission, and with bodybuilder ECW could build only for other state-owned fleets – Tilling, Scottish Bus and London Transport. Before this happened, in 1948, it was supplying chassis to export markets; this 1948 advert shows a Bristol L type chassis intended for an operator in India where it would be bodied locally. It would be 1965 before Bristol chassis and ECW bodies were available on the open market.

ECW was bodying complete buses for export markets, and this 1948 advert shows a 30ft (9.1m) long and 8ft (2.4m) wide bus, one of 50 on Bristol L chassis for 'various parts of the Union of South Africa'. The export activities of Bristol and ECW would cease the following year, after they passed into state ownership.

London orders

AEC, based in Southall, London, used what was very obviously a London Transport RT type AEC Regent to promote its range in this 1948 advert. The bus is a 1947 Park Royal-bodied delivery, complete with the roof number box that was specified on earlier RTs, but not used at the time of the photo as shortage of blind linen had resulted in the reduced destination display shown. AEC proudly and justifiably used the tagline 'Builders of London's Buses'.

MCW also saw the benefit in telling trade press readers in this 1949 advert that it had been 'entrusted with the building of some 2,000 bodies', in this case built for London Transport by Weymann at Addlestone.

Saunders Engineering and Shipyard, based at Beaumaris, on Anglesey, used this 1950 advert to announce an order for a further 50 bodies for London Transport, bringing its total to 300.

Opposite: Leyland, based in the town of Leyland in Lancashire, also picked up London orders. It supplied 1,631 Titan 7RTs for the RTL type, as well as the 500 8ft (2.4m) wide Titan 6RTs buses that made up the RTW type – the first London double-deckers to the recently approved width, as trumpeted in this 1948 advert featuring the Leyland types bought by London Transport and its 1906 predecessor.

Other chassis builders

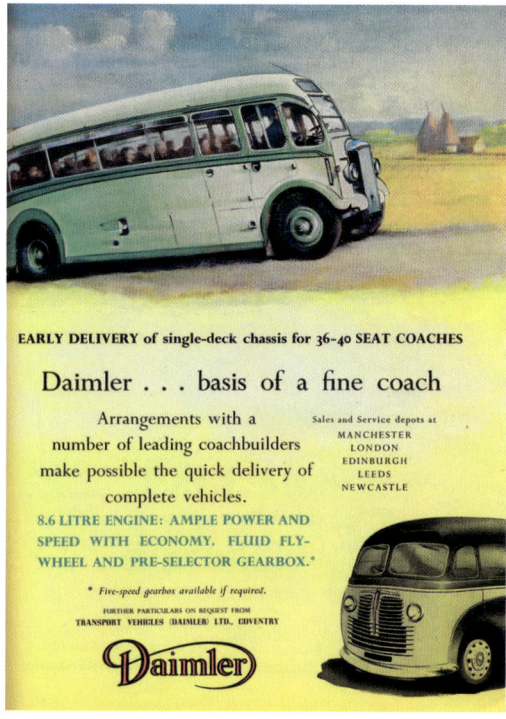

Few Daimler adverts around this time featured complete vehicles, but this 1950 advert shows a home market CVD6 with what looks like the inevitable Duple coach body, as well as an interesting export front end. Daimler pushed customers towards its own Coventry-built 8.6-litre engine, but many preferred the optional Gardner units, particularly for bus work, and the preselector gearbox was a strong selling point.

The Lancet III, built by Dennis at Guildford, was a 1945 reworking of a pre-war model and featured Dennis's own O.6 engine, which may have discouraged some potential customers used to the manufacturers' own engines in AECs, Daimlers and Leylands, as well as the popular Gardner range. This 1947 advert features a 1946 Santus-bodied example for Bowen of Birmingham. The accompanying text is of its time: 'Cab and control layout, being designed to conserve muscular energy, imparts to the driver a sure mastery that overcomes an emergency before it is able to mature'. Santus was based in Wigan.

Oldham-based truck maker Seddon entered the bus market in 1946 with the Perkins-engined Mk4 model, a sturdy chassis aimed at the home and export markets. This 1949 advert shows a Mk4 delivered to Cards of Devizes, posed alongside the RMS *Queen Elizabeth* at Southampton.

The Foden PVD range, built in Sandbach, sold in reasonable quantities between 1945 and 1956. This 1950 advert features a representation of one of eight Chester Corporation buses delivered between 1948 and 1951 with Massey bodies built in Wigan. The Chester livery was maroon and cream, but the restrictions of a second colour suggested a much brighter red.

Old looks and new looks

The 'new look' for double-deckers in the 1950s was the enclosed radiator, and a similar style of front was offered by Crossley, Daimler, Dennis and Guy. In 1950, Stockport-based Crossley was broadcasting the supply of 100 of these all-Crossley buses to Birmingham City Transport. As the advert reminds us, Crossley had already supplied 170 complete double-deckers to Birmingham, and it would supply more bodies on Daimler chassis in 1953–54. This style of bodywork was also built for Birmingham by Metro-Cammell.

Brush, based in Loughborough, was a very successful bus bodybuilder from the 1920s, and this advert, encouraging readers to visit its stand at the 1950 Commercial Motor Show, features a 1949 BMMO S9 40-seater. This would be the last appearance of Brush at a Commercial Motor Show, as it built its last buses in 1951.

A rare Park Royal advert from the years before it joined the ACV Group, featuring a pre-war Salford Corporation AEC Regent and the racehorse Windsor Lad. It was published in 1947, presumably before more up-to-date photos became available. Park Royal was based in north-west London.

Opposite: The 1948 two-colour advert for MCW shows a Sheffield AEC Regent III with attractive four-bay bodywork built by Weymann at Addlestone.

Bus bodybuilders

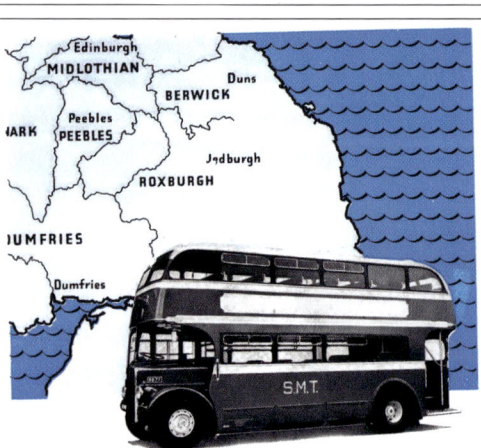

Northern Counties was only an occasional advertiser at this time. Based in Wigan, and mainly building double-deck bodies, it used a 1948 Douglas Corporation AEC Regent III delivery in this 1948 advert, emphasising the company's long experience supplying steel-framed bodies and highlighting its wartime performance, when it built 'every Steel Framed Double Deck Body built against the Government Civilian Omnibus Programme', something operators came to appreciate when Northern Counties utility bodies proved to be structurally much sounder than bodies from other builders using poor-quality timber.

Loughborough-based Willowbrook's adverts in the trade press at this time were straightforward and formulaic black-and-white adverts featuring a recent delivery. This 1950 advert shows a Trent Willowbrook-bodied 33-seat AEC Regal III.

While Duple was best-known as a builder of single-deck coach bodies, it also turned its hand to double-deckers, like this stylish four-bay body on a batch of 20 lowbridge 53-seaters for SMT in Edinburgh; similar bodies were built on Guy Arab III chassis for Red & White.

Opposite: Strachans, based in London, was another long-established bus bodybuilder, and the Aldershot & District company, as featured here in this 1948 advert, was a regular customer. This is a 1948 Dennis Lancet III with 32-seat rear entrance Strachan body. The Dennis/Strachans combination was popular with Aldershot & District.

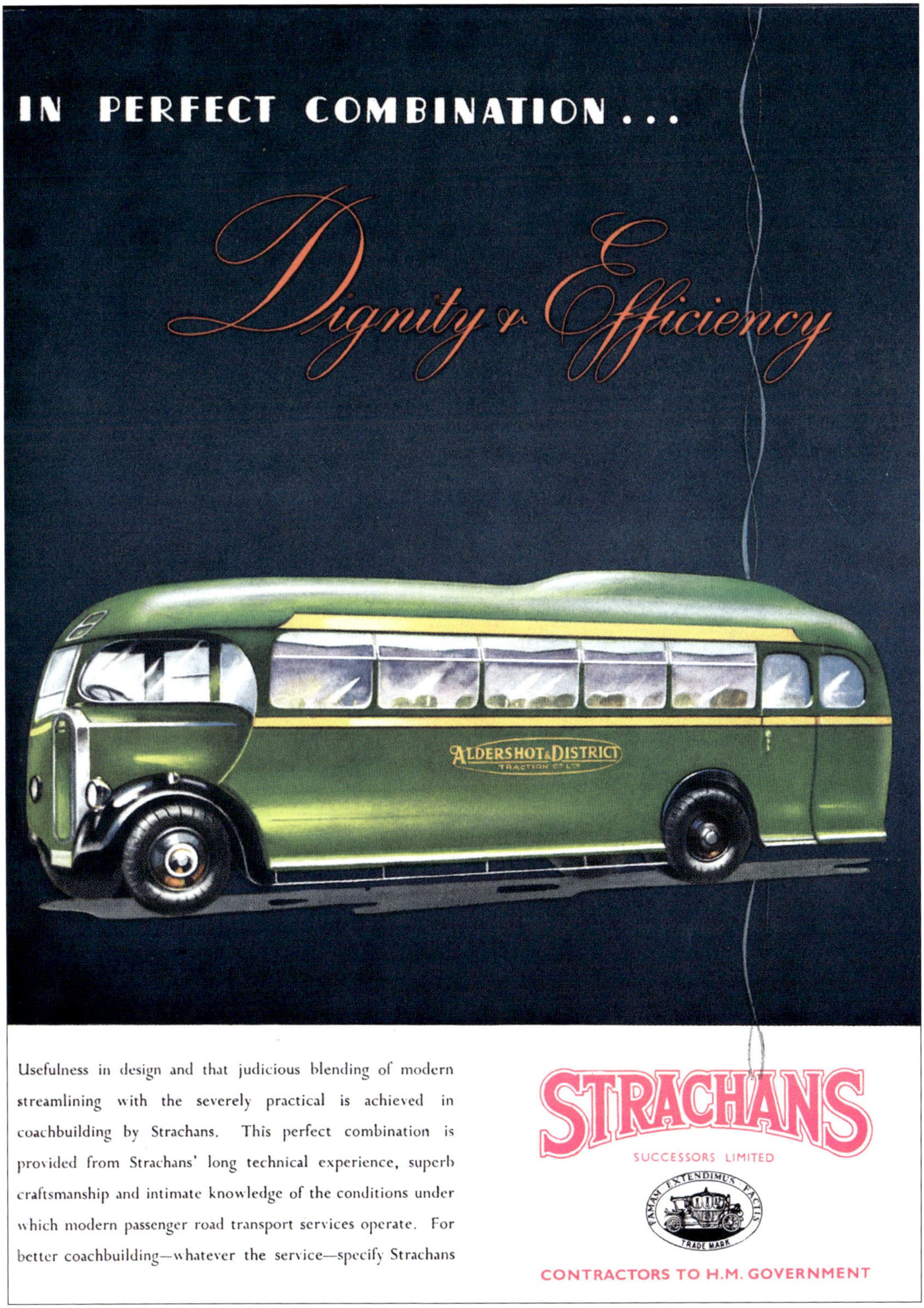

IN PERFECT COMBINATION...

Dignity & Efficiency

Usefulness in design and that judicious blending of modern streamlining with the severely practical is achieved in coachbuilding by Strachans. This perfect combination is provided from Strachans' long technical experience, superb craftsmanship and intimate knowledge of the conditions under which modern passenger road transport services operate. For better coachbuilding—whatever the service—specify Strachans

STRACHANS
SUCCESSORS LIMITED

CONTRACTORS TO H.M. GOVERNMENT

Chapter 3

1951–55
The Underfloor Revolution

The bus and coach builders that had worked hard to restart their businesses in the early post-war years, in the face of export commitments and a surge in passenger demand on the home front, had an opportunity to catch their breath in the early 1950s. Demand for new buses was starting to level off, and the new breed of underfloor-engined single-deck models allowed greater passenger capacity, particularly following the 1950 relaxation of the length regulations to 30ft (9.1m) for two-axle single-deckers, which meant these buses could seat up to 45 passengers, where 35 had often previously been the norm.

The trouble was that chassis manufacturers had gone down the route of developing sturdy big-engined chassis for their new underfloor-engined models that, with an equally sturdy body, meant that 45-seat single-deckers could weigh more than 56-seat double-deckers, burning at least as much fuel but carrying fewer passengers. Rising fuel costs led to demands from operators for lighter buses, and the main players rushed back to their drawing-boards to design a new lighter breed of models.

By 1953, AEC had its Reliance and Monocoach models, Guy had its Arab LUF and Leyland had its Tiger Cub, and many of the contemporary trade press adverts made great play of the fuel-saving potential of their offerings. The bodybuilders too looked at weight-saving, notably MCW, which had built lightweight double-deck bodies in 1939 and used its experience to develop the Orion model in the 1950s – much derided for its looks and basic finish, but unquestionably lightweight and unquestionably successful. Body weights of less than two tons were quoted in advertising.

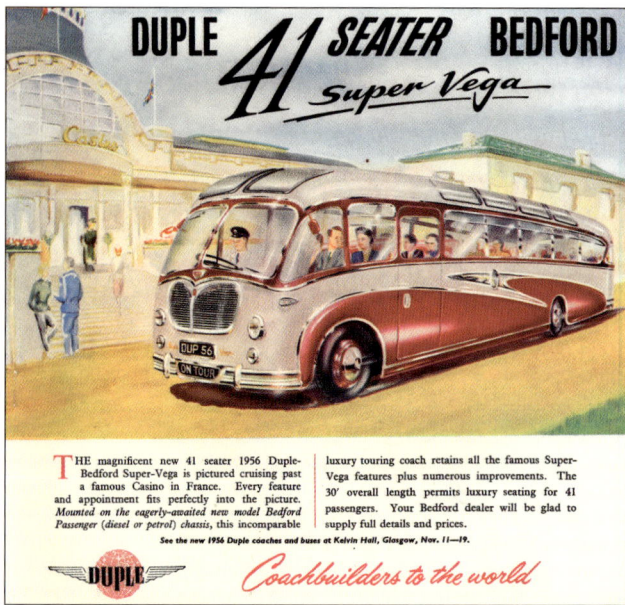

Left: Bedford and Duple continued to dominate the lightweight coach market in the early 1950s, after Bedford upgraded from the little OB chassis to what it called the 'Big Bedfords'. This SB with exaggerated Duple Super Vega body appeared in this 1955 Duple advert, promoting its 1956 body range.

Opposite left: 1950s adverts sometimes introduced historical references, like this 1952 Dunlopillo advert with an early London General Orion bus contrasting with one of London Transport's latest RT-type AEC Regents.

Opposite right: MCW also dug into the past with this 1955 advert, which also used a 1905 London General Orion, in this case to compare with a 1955 Maidstone & District Leyland Titan PD2 with MCW's lightweight Orion bodywork.

1951–55: The Underfloor Revolution

The new underfloor-engined single-deck models quickly signalled the end of their heavier front-engined predecessors, but in the lightweight market full-size front-engined models like Bedford's market-leading SB range continued to sell well to coach operators of all sizes, as well as to bus operators wanting to reduce their costs on less remunerative routes.

These years also saw the disappearance of many of the smaller bodybuilders that had grasped the opportunities of the post-war years but now found that their orders had dried up. Some diversified, some merged and some simply closed down. And there was one major name – Brush – that pulled out of bus bodybuilding to concentrate on what were potentially more lucrative activities.

The main chassis builders – AEC, Daimler Guy and Leyland – continued to place regular adverts in the trade press, as did bodybuilders Duple, MCW, Park Royal and Willowbrook, but manufacturers that would become increasingly important, like Dennis, Burlingham, Harrington and Plaxtons, still appeared to be saving their advertising budgets until they had significant new models to promote.

Two very successful models that would go into production in the late 1950s had their roots in experimental models that first took to the streets in the early 1950s. London Transport's Routemaster, successor to the fabled RT family and originally conceived to replace London's trolleybuses, first appeared in prototype form in 1954 but only went into production in 1958, and in their advertising in the trade press its builders lost no opportunity to remind readers exactly who had been entrusted with the task, as we shall see in the next chapter.

Leyland was exploring the concept of rear-engined double-deckers and in 1954 built an experimental chassis, the Low Floor Double Deck Bus Chassis, shortened to LFDD (but also unofficially known as the Lowloader), which did the rounds of potential customers and eventually emerged as the Atlantean in 1956. The rather different production model, like the Routemaster, went into production in 1958.

Although longer single-deckers had been legalised, it would take a little more time until longer double-deckers could appear, and operators could take advantage of an increase in seating capacity from around 64 to a potential 78, which with passenger numbers starting to drop and fuel prices continuing to rise, was high on their wish-lists.

Double-deck variety

Leyland liked to pepper its adverts with figures and statistics to demonstrate how sturdy, economical and popular its products were. This 1952 advert shows a newly-delivered Titan PD2 delivered to Yorkshire Traction, with Leyland's own 58-seat body – Leyland did tend to feature its own bodies in its adverts. But not for much longer, as Leyland stopped building bus bodies in 1954. This advert highlights good fuel consumption and bodies that 'show surprisingly little deterioration, even after 300,000 miles or more'. Buses like this typically weighed almost 8 tons, and soon a new breed of much lighter bodies came along.

Leeds-based Roe had been building bus bodies since the 1920s, and in 1948 with sister coachbuilder Park Royal it became part of the new ACV Group in 1948. Roe's reputation was based on well-built composite constructed bodies like the AEC Regent III in this 1952 advert, one of hundreds of bodies built for Leeds City Transport over the years.

The ACV Group ran a series of Proud Association colour adverts in the trade press in the 1950s, featuring buses from some of the more prestigious fleets. This 1952 ad featured one of the hundreds of Crossley-bodied Crossley DD42s delivered to Birmingham City Transport in 1949/50; the last 100 deliveries introduced the 'new-look' front worn by the bus in this 1952 advert.

Truck builder Atkinson of Walton-le-Dale dabbled in the bus market in the 1950s and 1960s, with models powered by the engineers' favourite Gardner engines. Its single-deck models enjoyed some success, and in 1954 it launched its PD746 double-deck chassis with Gardner 6LW engine. Just one was sold, fitted with a Northern Counties centre-entrance body for SHMD Board, but for this 1954 advert the artist had concocted a rather outdated and unconvincing body on a photo of the chassis. The 1955 photo shows the real thing, with a Northern Counties body, unusually with a centre entrance. This bus is now preserved.

Single-deck buses

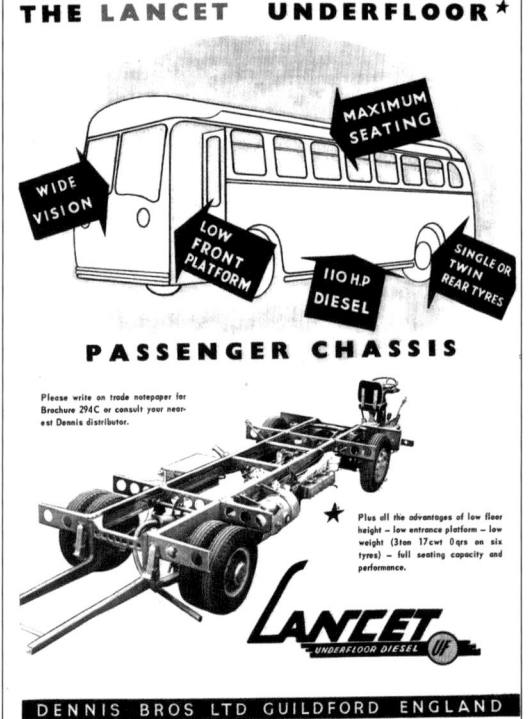

The first underfloor-engined single-deck models from AEC, Daimler, Guy and Leyland were heavyweights, and while they sold well in export markets, home operators started agitating for much lighter types. The Daimler Freeline never achieved the level of sales of its underfloor-engined competitors, but loyal Daimler customers like Swindon Corporation bought four of these with 34-seat centre entrance bodies in 1954, featured here by Park Royal in 1954 in its regular advert style – although unlike this one, the chassis of many of the buses featured came from fellow ACV Group companies.

Atkinson's brief foray into bus building included the Alpha PL745H chassis with Gardner 5HLW engine, here in a 1953 Willowbrook advert featuring a North Western rear-entrance example, weighing a commendable 5 ton 8cwt (5567kg). The Willowbrook logo includes a reference to Brush patents, and the text describes the 'Willowbrook-Brush Light Alloy body'; Willowbrook had acquired the patents for Brush metal-framed bodies in 1952.

Dennis introduced its Lancet UF chassis in 1953 with its horizontal O.6 engine, but sales were disappointing. Another two Dennis underfloor chassis types – the heavyweight Dominant in 1950 and the lightweight Pelican in 1956 – never got beyond the prototype stage.

Opposite: AEC's heavyweight offering was the Regal IV, only identified as such in the caption to the small photo. Otherwise, it was the 'A.C.V. Mark IV' in this 1952 advert. The bus threading its way through the traffic represents a Roe-bodied example.

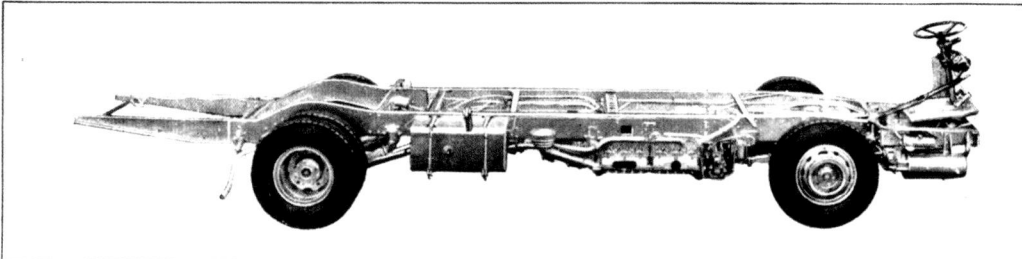

A.C.V. advanced chassis design gives ....

greater manœuvrability

The advanced chassis design of the A.C.V. Mk. IV gives greater manœuvrability due to a shorter wheelbase. This design, with its underfloor engine, brings other advantages, too: it provides greater comfort for a larger number of passengers; quieter travelling — the engine noise is much less audible; and improved suspension — the passenger load is more evenly distributed.

Among the A.C.V. vehicles operated by GARNERS COACHES LTD., London, W.5, is this smart underfloor engine, Regal Mark IV.

 A.C.V. MARK IV SINGLE DECK **PASSENGER CHASSIS** WITH UNDERFLOOR ENGINE

The A.C.V. Group of Companies includes A.E.C., Crossley Motors and the Maudslay Motor Co. Its sales organisation is
A.C.V. SALES LTD., 49 BERKELEY SQUARE, LONDON, W.1 Telephone: REGent 2141.

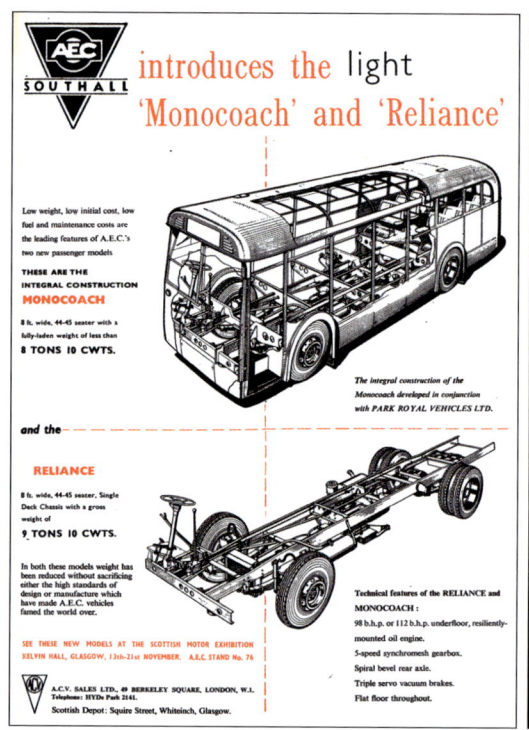

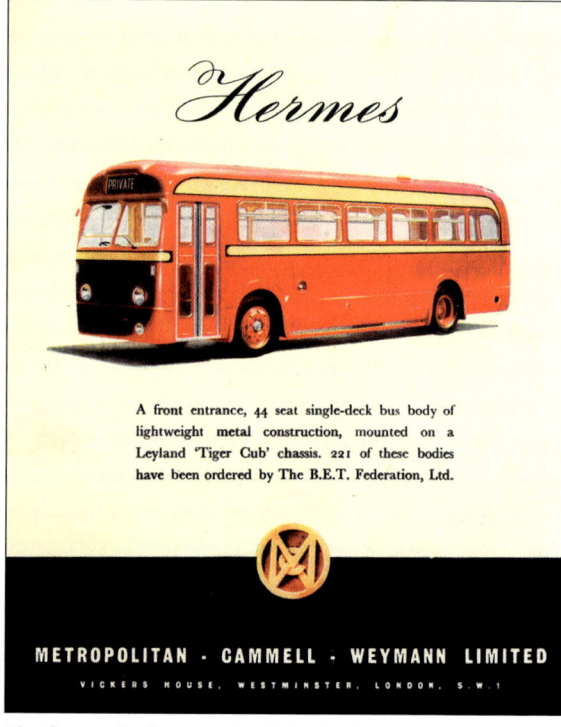

The first underfloor-engined single-deck buses from the mainstream manufacturers had been heavyweight models but increasing concerns about fuel costs sent designers back to their drawing-boards to produce new ranges of considerably lighter types. AEC hedged its bets with two technically similar variations – the Monocoach and Reliance. The Monocoach was a chassisless integral bus, normally completed by Park Royal, as shown. The Reliance was a chassis for bus and coach bodies from any builder. In practice, the Monocoach was popular with a small selection of home market operators while the Reliance went on to great sales success and remained in production until 1979. Integrally constructed vehicles tended to be lighter, and the fully laden weight of the Monocoach was a full ton lighter than a bodied Reliance.

MCW's standard single-deck bus offering in the 1950s was the Hermes, seen here on a Leyland Tiger Cub chassis in this 1954 advert representing an order from the BET Group for 221 bodies. In 1951, MCW was promoting this style of body with just 27 seats and space for 35 standees, with a conductor's cash desk and two doors for passengers to board (rear) and alight. The bus featured is in fact a Glasgow Corporation 1950 BUT RETB1 trolleybus, bodied by Weymann at Addlestone.

Opposite: Saunders-Roe at Anglesey developed the attractive lightweight Saro body for Leyland's Tiger Cub chassis, and this sold well to companies in the BET Group. In this 1953 advert, Saunders-Roe claims to be 'builders of the world's lightest bodies'.

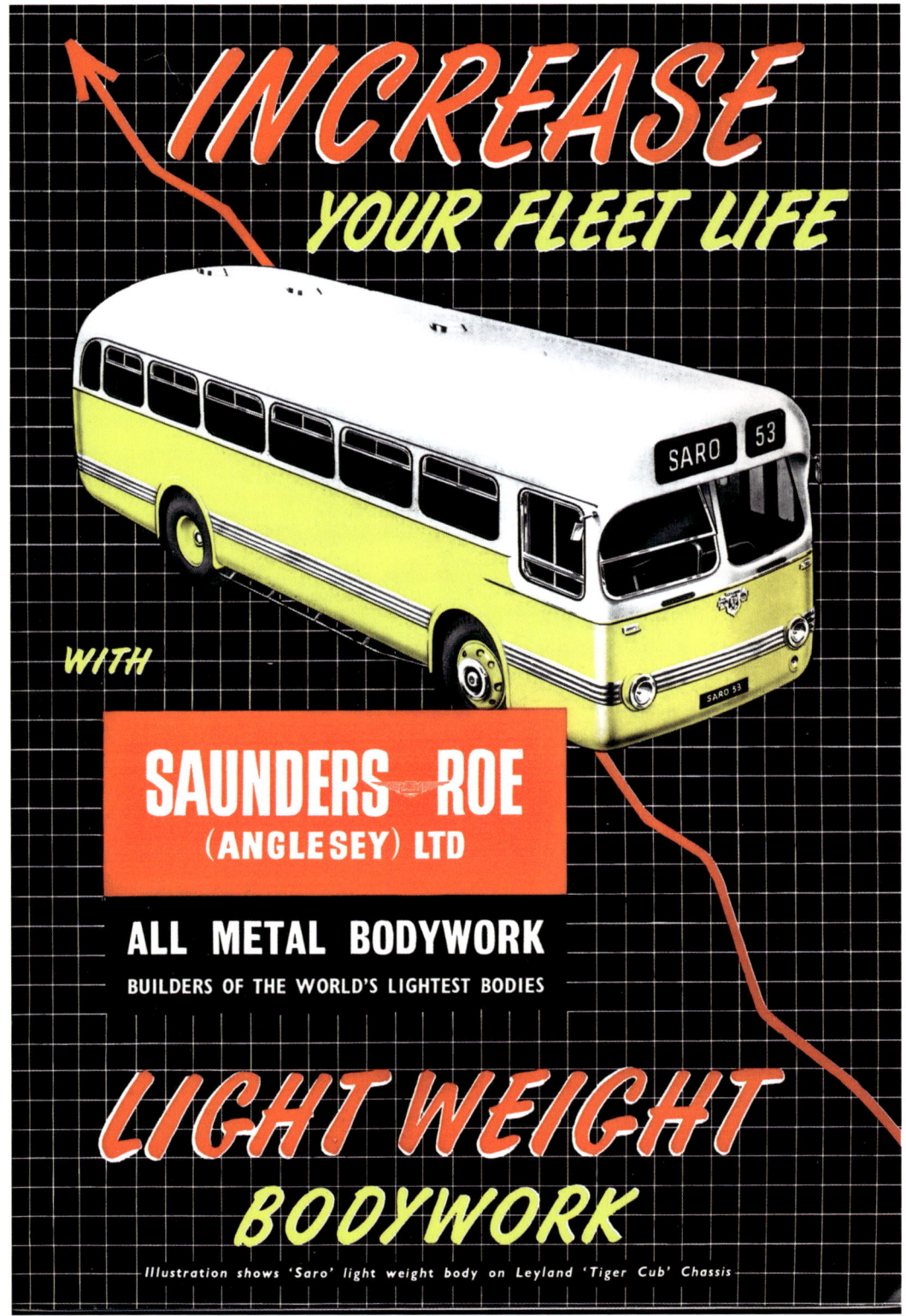

Lightweight coaches

The Leyland Tiger Cub was first promoted as a lightweight chassis for service bus bodies, and from 1954 Leyland was highlighting the more powerful coach version for the 1954 season, here with Alexander bodywork. Although Alexander, based at Stirling at this time, was by this stage still working to attract new orders, it rarely saw the need to advertise in the trade press.

The Plaxtons coachbuilding business was still way behind Duple in the 1950s, and unlike Duple it rarely advertised its products. This 1953 advert shows the 1954 version of its Venturer body, mounted on Bedford SB chassis.

The adverts placed by Yeates of Loughborough were almost as flashy as the bodies it produced. Hardly a shrinking violet, this is a 1953 advert for the well-chromed Riviera body on AEC Reliance for the Robin Hood fleet.

Opposite: Many operators moved up from the Bedford OB/Duple Vista combination to what were promoted as the Big Bedfords, like this 1955-model SB type with Super Vega body in a 1954 Duple advert.

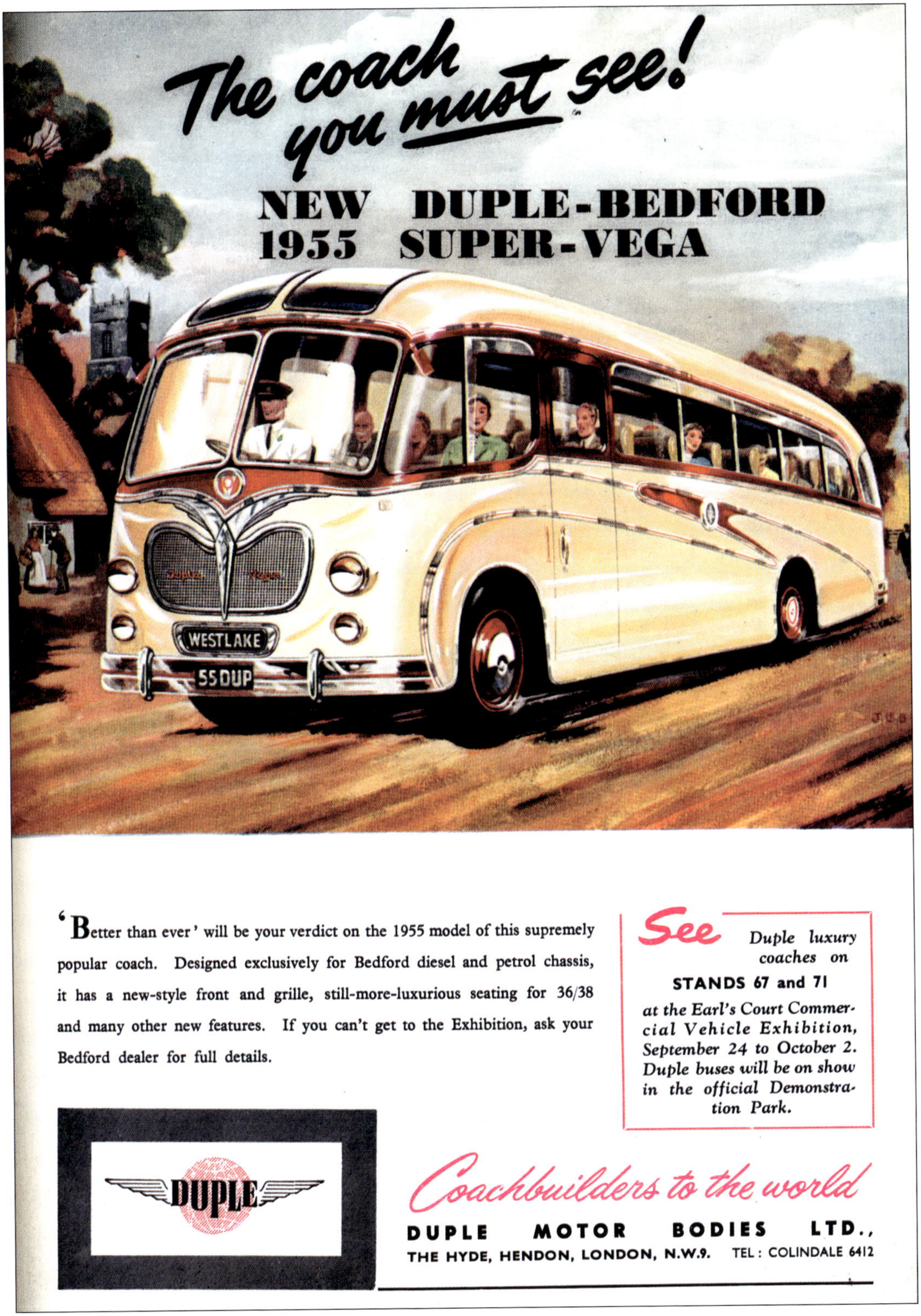

The coach you must see!

NEW DUPLE-BEDFORD 1955 SUPER-VEGA

'**B**etter than ever' will be your verdict on the 1955 model of this supremely popular coach. Designed exclusively for Bedford diesel and petrol chassis, it has a new-style front and grille, still-more-luxurious seating for 36/38 and many other new features. If you can't get to the Exhibition, ask your Bedford dealer for full details.

See Duple luxury coaches on **STANDS 67 and 71** at the Earl's Court Commercial Vehicle Exhibition, September 24 to October 2. Duple buses will be on show in the official Demonstration Park.

Coachbuilders to the world
DUPLE MOTOR BODIES LTD.,
THE HYDE, HENDON, LONDON, N.W.9.   TEL: COLINDALE 6412

Heavier coaches

The first underfloor-engined coaches were built on the original heavyweight chassis introduced by the leading players. This substantial looking coach, imagined outside the Brighton Pavilion in this 1953 advert, is a Duple Coronation Ambassador for Southdown on Leyland Royal Tiger chassis. 'With its air of streamlined majesty and luxurious interior, it strikes the right note for Coronation Year!', according to the copywriter.

Southdown had previously been a customer for Duple's rather simpler Ambassador body, as seen here in a 1953 Leyland advert featuring a 1952 Royal Tiger, although the familiar Southdown green livery has been sacrificed to the blue second colour available for that page in the trade magazine.

Leyland also produced its own bodywork for the Royal Tiger, a distinctive shape that proved popular with some of its larger customers. In this 1953 advert, Leyland reels off figures – 40 per cent of customers have come back for a second time for Royal Tigers, 14 per cent for a third time and 9 per cent for a fourth time.

Opposite: Roe was primarily a builder of service bus bodies, but like most bodybuilders it produced coaches from time to time, sometimes at the request of regular customers. This is a body style built for Lancashire United in 1952, a centre entrance 39-seater on Guy Arab UF chassis, although the illustration in the advert seems to suggest that it is on an AEC chassis built by a fellow ACV Group member.

All types of Single and Double Deck Omnibus and Coach Bodies

ROE
Craftsmen Coachbuilders.

CHARLES H. ROE LIMITED, CROSSGATES, LEEDS
Telephone 45182

Coach variety

Above: A novel and attractive way to provide seating and luggage space for airline passengers was this 37-seat design with lower seats at the front and seats raised over a luggage compartment towards the rear. London Transport operated 65 of these, built in 1952–53 on AEC Regal IV chassis, on behalf of British European Airways (BEA) to carry airline passengers and their luggage between London termini and London's airports. This 1953 Park Royal advert includes the usual indication at the lower part showing the Park Royal works and a representation of the range of body types produced – buses, trolleybuses, single-deckers, export vehicles and even diesel railcars. And of course, a BEA coach.

Opposite: Coachbuilders were still busy rebodying older chassis, particularly relatively recent half-cab buses that many operators felt now looked old-fashioned following the spread of full-fronted buses and coaches in the 1950s. Duple was advertising its ability to modernise fleets in 1954 – 'turn in your old coaches at the end of the traffic season, have a smart new fleet for the next – and save enormously!'. This was a 1947 AEC Regal chassis from the London Timpson coaching business that had been new with a Vincent body and was effectively modernised in 1954 to appear not unlike a contemporary Bedford/Duple product.

Foden broke new ground with its PVR chassis, with its transverse engine mounted low at the rear. This 1952 advert features a Bellhouse Hartwell-bodied PVRF6 and the headline 'The REAR Engine has put the forward engine BEHIND for all time'. While in 1952 the trend was towards underfloor-mounted engines, which were admittedly behind forward engines, it would be another decade before rear-engined single-deck buses and coaches became more familiar. Bellhouse Hartwell bodies were built in Bolton.

Mann Egerton of Norwich became sole licensees for the Crellin-Duplex Half-Deck coach, an unusual body design that allowed 50 passengers to be carried, where a conventional coach might have 41 seats. This advert appeared in 1952, anticipating the Coronation festivities of 1953, and featured an AEC Regal IV supplied to Ripponden & District. Few were sold.

Harrington, based in Hove, was a long-established and well-respected coachbuilder with many regular customers. This 1952 advert features a 26-seat touring coach, one of 20 built on Leyland Royal Tiger chassis for Southdown.

Bodybuilder miscellany

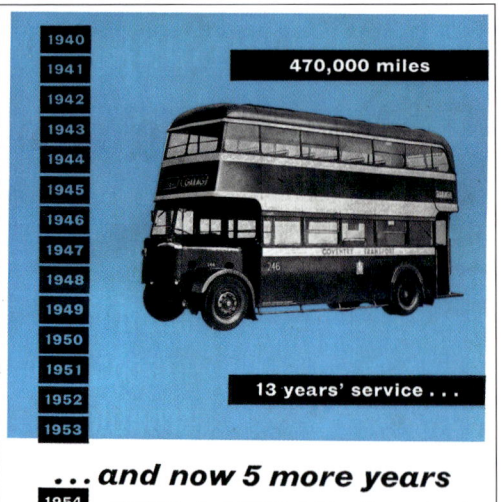

In 1953, to promote its new lightweight Orion body, MCW used this advert showing a 1940 Coventry Corporation delivery that had completed 470,000 miles in 13 years and in 1953 was 'certified roadworthy and approved for another five years' service'.

Refurbishment of wartime bodies continued into the early 1950s, and this Willowbrook 1952 advert demonstrates how effective this can be, showing two North Western Guy Arabs side by side; the bus on the left carries its original Roe utility lowbridge body, and on the right is a similar bus after the Willowbrook treatment.

Burlingham, hardly a regular advertiser at this time, used its September 1952 pre-Commercial Motor Show advert as a teaser to encourage potential customers to visit stand 24 to see what was under the dust sheet. The red hand should perhaps be facing the curious gentleman rather than the reader.

Opposite: For its December 1954 advert, Park Royal sent Christmas wishes to its friends, with line drawings showing the wide range of its products – an East Kent Guy Arab IV double-decker, a Northern General AEC Monocoach single-deck bus, and a Birch Bros AEC Reliance with its new Royalist coach body. Park Royal concentrated on service bus bodies but occasionally dipped a toe in the luxury coach market. The Royalist, closely resembling ECW's contemporary coach body, was not a big seller.

Weight-saving

As concerns grew among bus operators about fuel costs, chassis and bodybuilders rushed to strip weight out of their range. MCW had a head start, as it had been producing lighter all-metal bodies since 1939. The 1952 prototype MCW Orion body on Daimler CLG5 chassis for Potteries Motor Traction is featured in this 1953 advert. The body weight, we are told, was just 1 ton 16cwt (1,849kg), which for a 58-seat body was impressive, while the unladen weight of the bus was just over 6 tons.

Burlingham, best known for its Blackpool-built coach range, also produced service bus bodies, like this 1954 example on Leyland Tiger Cub chassis for Baxter's of Airdrie. The 1954 advert trumpets the body weight of 1 ton 17cwt (1,909kg) for a 44-seat bus.

Leyland's fondness for including figures in its advertising is again evident in this 1953 advert for its new Tiger Cub model, quoting loading times on a 44-seat Tiger Cub that were lower than on a 35-seater, adding that the Tiger Cub fuel consumption was 2mpg less than the smaller bus. The illustration shows a Weymann-bodied bus.

Opposite: Edinburgh Corporation was an early customer for MCW's Orion, building up a fleet of 300 Orion-bodied Leyland Titan PD2s in the mid-1950s. This 1955 Leyland advert highlights the unladen weight of 6 ton 12cwt (6,807kg) and the average fuel consumption of 10.53mpg. To achieve the low body weight, the Edinburgh Orions had basic interiors lacking the ornate trim of many contemporary deliveries.

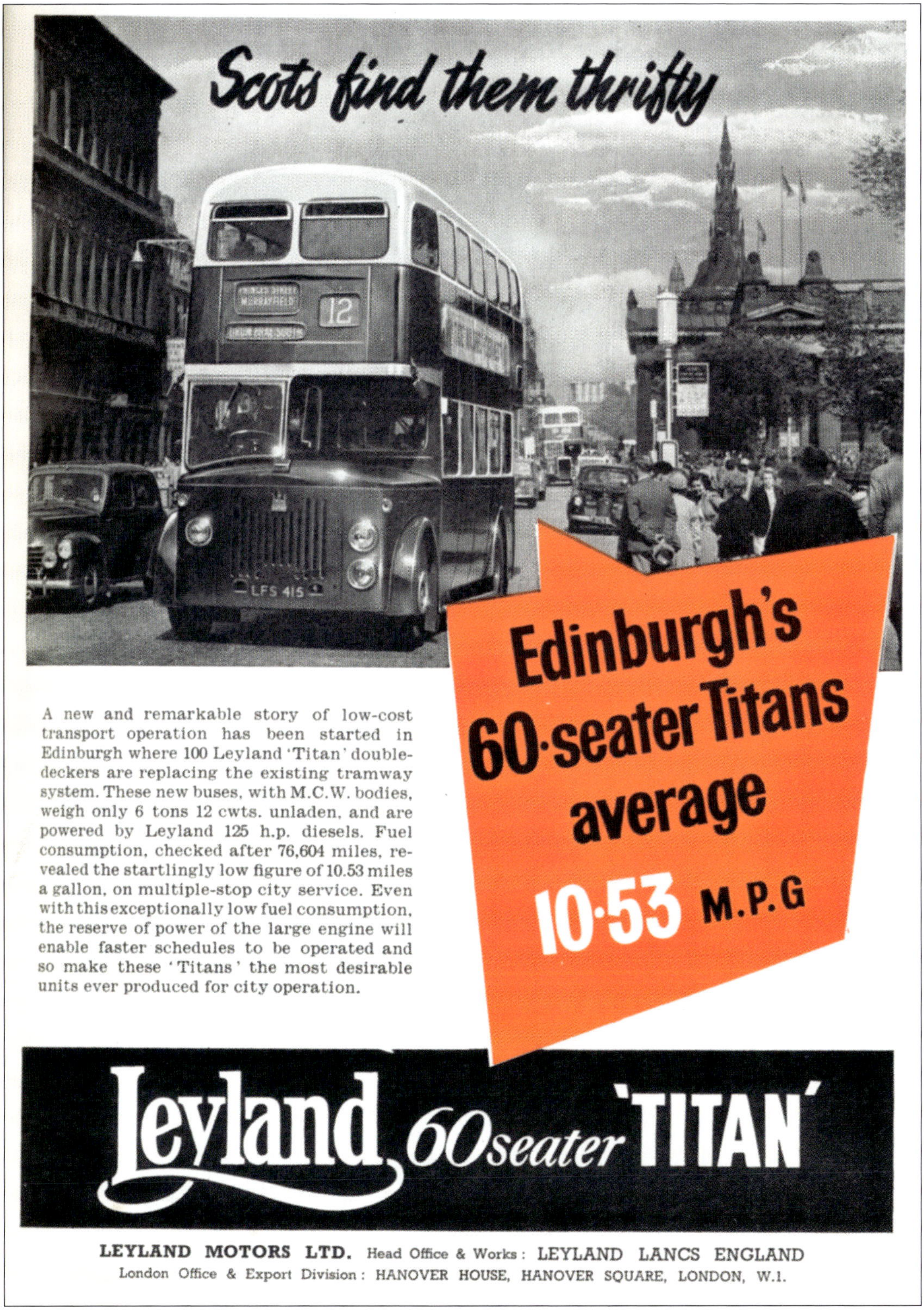
Scots find them thrifty
12
LFS 415
Edinburgh's 60-seater Titans average 10·53 M.P.G
A new and remarkable story of low-cost transport operation has been started in Edinburgh where 100 Leyland 'Titan' double-deckers are replacing the existing tramway system. These new buses, with M.C.W. bodies, weigh only 6 tons 12 cwts. unladen, and are powered by Leyland 125 h.p. diesels. Fuel consumption, checked after 76,604 miles, revealed the startlingly low figure of 10.53 miles a gallon, on multiple-stop city service. Even with this exceptionally low fuel consumption, the reserve of power of the large engine will enable faster schedules to be operated and so make these 'Titans' the most desirable units ever produced for city operation.
Leyland 60seater 'TITAN'
LEYLAND MOTORS LTD. Head Office & Works: LEYLAND LANCS ENGLAND
London Office & Export Division: HANOVER HOUSE, HANOVER SQUARE, LONDON, W.1.

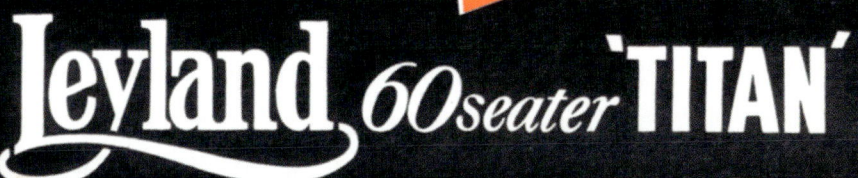

Chapter 4
1956–60 Double-Deck Developments

By the mid-1950s, the concept of lightweight underfloor-engined single-deck buses was well established, and the luxury coach market was split between the less expensive lighter-weight front-engined models from Bedford and Commer, and the more substantial, but still relatively lightweight, underfloor types from AEC, Guy and Leyland. The first part of what grew into the M6 motorway was opened in 1958, and operators of express coach services started looking for more powerful types that would handle sustained higher speeds, so AEC uprated its Reliance and Leyland created its new Leopard model.

Relaxation of the legal length of double-deckers in 1956 signalled the start of a new era of high-capacity types. The increase from a 27ft (8.2m) maximum to 30ft (9.1m) meant that double-deckers

Above left: The revolutionary big-windowed Panorama body propelled Plaxton into the big league of coachbuilders. This was the first example (which became the overall winner at the 1958 Brighton Coach Rally) in an AEC 1958 advert that name-checks its Reliance chassis five times, but just mentions Plaxton once. The coach was for Sheffield United Tours.

Above right: Commer was Bedford's main competitor for the lightweight coach chassis market in the 1950s. This 1956 Duple advert shows a Commer Avenger fitted with the distinctive-sounding Rootes two-stroke TS3 diesel engine.

could initially carry up to ten extra passengers, and many operators grasped this opportunity, although some continued to favour the 27ft (8.2m) models. AEC, Daimler, Guy and Leyland quickly created longer versions of their existing models, as did Bristol for the state-owned sector.

Then Leyland, which had been experimenting with rear-engined models for some years, took advantage of the length relaxation to launch its new 78-seat Atlantean, an integral bus produced with MCW. This bus totally reinvented the double-deck bus concept, and although the integral Atlantean was not what operators wanted, when it reappeared in 1958 as a separate chassis, the future shape of double-deckers was defined for the next 40 years. Front-engined double-deckers were by no means dead in the late 1950s, as several operators stuck with what they knew, and they would survive on the model lists for just over a decade.

London Transport, as often was the case, ploughed a different furrow and created the 27ft 6in (8.4m)-long Routemaster, which after a long gestation period went into full production in 1958. Defiantly front-engined and with many advanced features, it was designed for speed and manoeuvrability in London traffic and spawned 30ft (9.1m) versions and even a single rear-engined prototype.

The success of the Bristol Lodekka in a market restricted to state-owned fleets encouraged other British manufacturers to produce similar models. AEC and Park Royal combined to offer the integral Bridgemaster in 1956; Leyland would introduce its Lowlander in 1961, badged as an Albion for Scottish customers; and Dennis negotiated with Bristol to build the Lodekka under licence. AEC would later introduce a lowheight chassis, the Renown, but none of these models could mirror the success of the Lodekka and may have been rather late to the party.

Bus and coach operators were now agitating for longer single-deckers, some as a more flexible alternative to double-deckers, but had to wait until 1961 before they could buy any.

Above left: The Albion Aberdonian was a lighter and simpler version of the Tiger Cub – Albion, based in Clydebank, Glasgow, had been part of the Leyland group since 1951. This 1958 advert shows a 1957 North Western delivery with Weymann body.

Above right: Most artists' impressions exaggerated the appearance of the buses or coaches portrayed, but this 1957 Dennis advert for the Loline, which would be built under licence from Bristol, hardly does it justice, as if the artist may not have actually looked at a bus for some time.

Coaching luxury

Duple and Bedford still dominated the lightweight coach market, with frequent facelifts to the bodywork to keep the designs fresh and encourage operators to buy the latest version. Duple's 1960 Super Vega on Bedford SB chassis was very different from its 1957 predecessor. According to this 1960 advert 'She's sleek, she's graceful… she's got the kind of good-looks passengers go for.'

Harrington, based in Hove, enjoyed great success with its Cavalier and later Grenadier bodies. This 1959 advert used an artist's impression, which, for once, may not have done justice to what turned out to be an impressive and popular design. Harrington bodies had sold well to a faithful band of customers, but its Cavalier body, announced in 1959, brought its products into a much wider range of fleets.

At this time, Plaxtons was beginning to gnaw away at Duple's dominance, but was an infrequent advertiser, sticking to black-and-white. This 1956 advert promotes the 1957 Consort range on Bedford, Commer and underfloor-engined chassis.

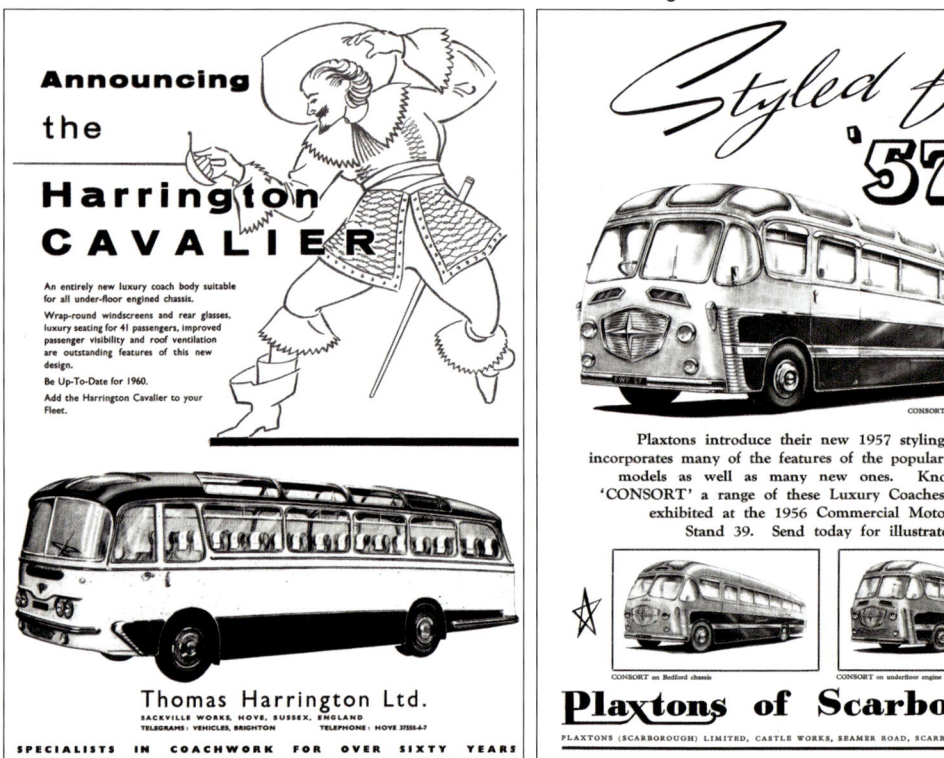

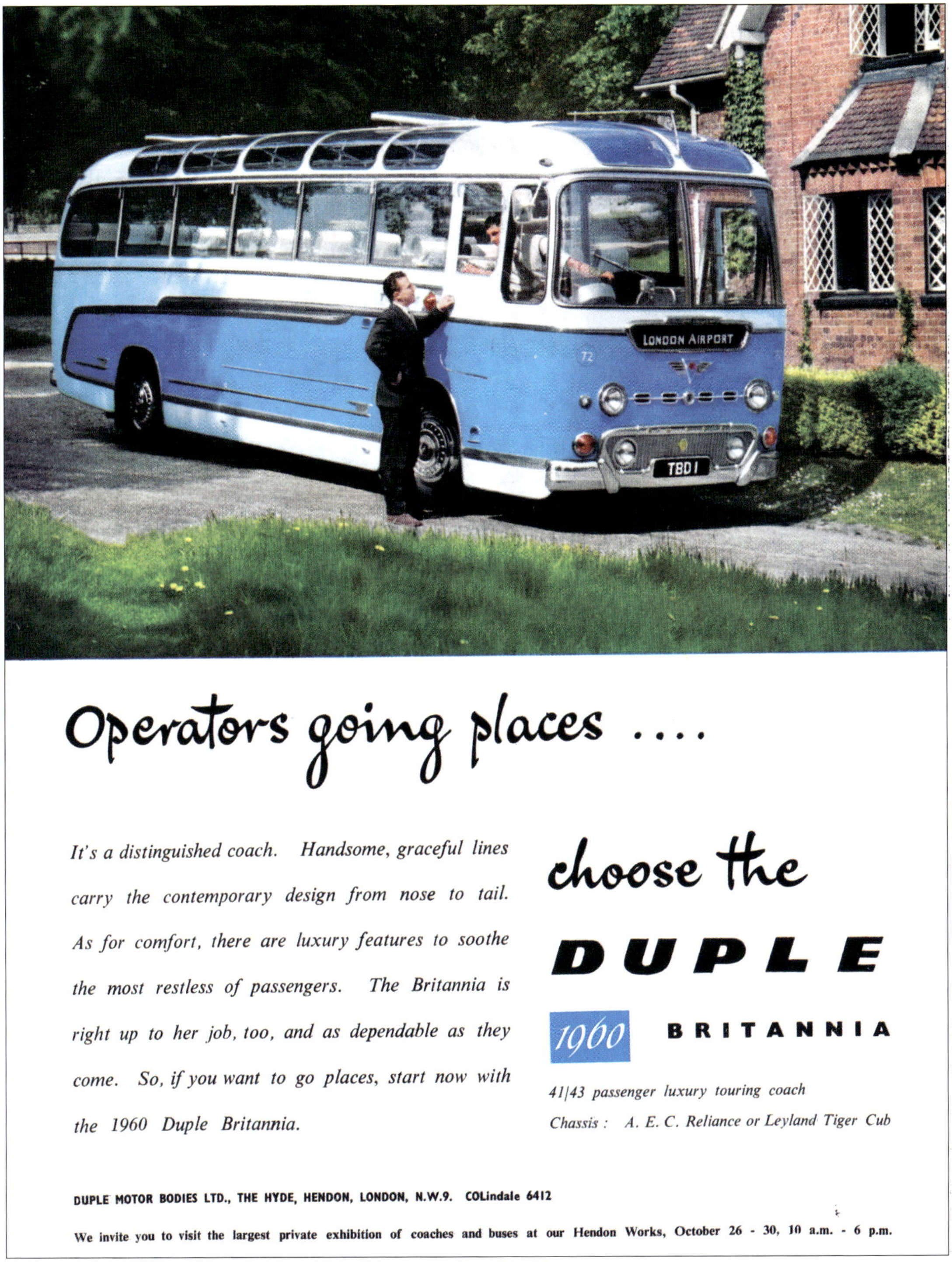
LONDON AIRPORT
TBD 1
Operators going places ....
It's a distinguished coach. Handsome, graceful lines carry the contemporary design from nose to tail. As for comfort, there are luxury features to soothe the most restless of passengers. The Britannia is right up to her job, too, and as dependable as they come. So, if you want to go places, start now with the 1960 Duple Britannia.
choose the
DUPLE
1960
BRITANNIA
41/43 passenger luxury touring coach
Chassis : A. E. C. Reliance or Leyland Tiger Cub
DUPLE MOTOR BODIES LTD., THE HYDE, HENDON, LONDON, N.W.9. COLindale 6412
We invite you to visit the largest private exhibition of coaches and buses at our Hendon Works, October 26 - 30, 10 a.m. - 6 p.m.

The 1960 Duple Britannia, advertised here late in 1959, was an attractive coach for underfloor-engined chassis – seen here on an AEC Reliance for York Bros of Northampton.

In this 1957 advert, Leyland claimed to be the 'pioneer of big-capacity low-weight coaches', showing an East Midland 1954 Tiger Cub with Burlingham Seagull body. Although Burlingham was a successful bus and coach bodybuilder, it rarely advertised its own wares in the trade press.

Leyland identified a demand for more a powerful single-deck chassis and introduced the Leopard, which combined the Tiger Cub frame with the O.600 engine. This 1960 advert features a 1959 Sheffield Joint Omnibus Committee example with 30ft (9.1m) long Weymann Fanfare body, but the Leopard would come into its own the following year when buses up to 36ft (11m) long were legalised in Britain.

As part of the Rootes Group since 1952, Beadle offered a range of Beadle-Commer integral buses and coaches, incorporating the Rootes two-stroke diesel engine, but production ceased in 1957, a year after this advert was published. It features the Rochester coach on a Kent tour passing typical Kentish oast houses; Beadle was based in Dartford, Kent.

Opposite: Alexander developed this style for underfloor-engined chassis in the 1950s, and it was built on AEC, Albion, Guy and Leyland chassis. This is a 1957 Albion Aberdonian for Western SMT in a 1957 Albion advert.

Here comes the
ABERDONIAN
41 SEATER
AOA
Western
K11384
KCS 423
And at the right price too
KERBSIDE WEIGHT 5½ TONS
LOW RUNNING COSTS
ATTRACTIVE INITIAL COST
Economy from the word go. That's the feature of the new Albion ABERDONIAN — the lightweight coach with the big capacity and with an initial cost that is keenly competitive.
Independent road tests carried out by a number of the technical press have shown a fuel consumption of 20 m.p.g. under coaching conditions with a full load when averaging 30 m.p.h. With a kerbside weight of only 5½ tons it can seat 41 passengers in luxurious comfort.
Immensely robust, scientifically designed and with a very favourable power-weight ratio, the ABERDONIAN will keep running costs down to rock bottom while maintaining the highest standard of operational efficiency.
It is powered by the famous Leyland 6-cylinder 95 h.p. horizontal engine, and fitted with Albion's well tried overhead worm drive transmission and a powerful, efficient brake system–vacuum hydraulically operated.
In fact the ABERDONIAN *has* more, *gives* more, and *does* more than any other vehicle of similar capacity–on either urban bus routes or long distance coach service.
Albion
MOTORS LIMITED
SCOTSTOUN, GLASGOW, W.4
Home Sales Office: 3 LYGON PLACE, LONDON, S.W.1. Tel: SLOane 6117
Export Division: HANOVER HOUSE, HANOVER SQUARE, LONDON, W.1. Tel: MAYfair 8561

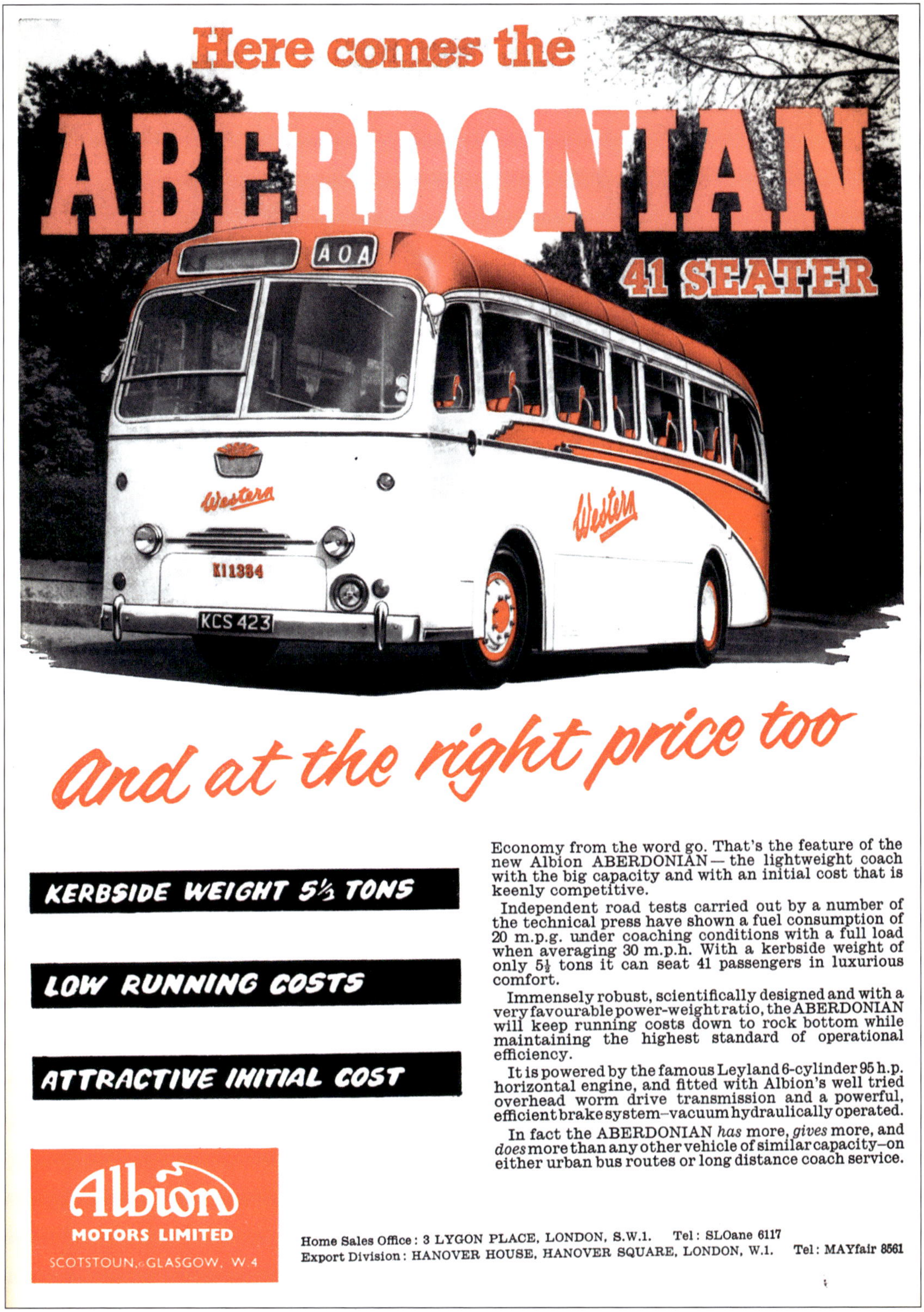

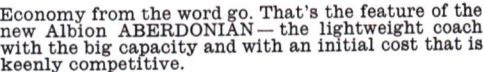

Single-deck buses

Economy was still the watchword in the early 1960s, and AEC promoted 'Single-deck economy with double-deck power' in this 1958 advert showing a 1957 Reading Corporation Reliance with Burlingham two-door bodywork mopping up a load of younger schoolchildren. It is one-man-operated 42-seater.

Plaxtons was principally a coach builder, but, like its competitors, it built bus bodies in the summer months to keep its factory busy after the new coaches for the season had taken to the road – Plaxtons here offering delivery from 1 July. The artist's impression shows an AEC Reliance with Plaxtons' Highway 45-seat body.

In 1958, Leyland was advertising its Tiger Cub model with 'the famous' Leyland Pneumo-Cyclic gearbox with two-pedal control, providing what to many drivers would have been a welcome change from Leyland's constant mesh box. The bus featured is a Trent 1954 Weymann-bodied example.

Opposite: Duple's straight-waisted and bus-like Donington body was built at its Duple (Midland) facility at Kegworth and was a useful dual-purpose type for bus and coach duties. This 1957 advert shows a Donington on Leyland Tiger Cub chassis showing its destination as Hendon, home of Duple's main factory.

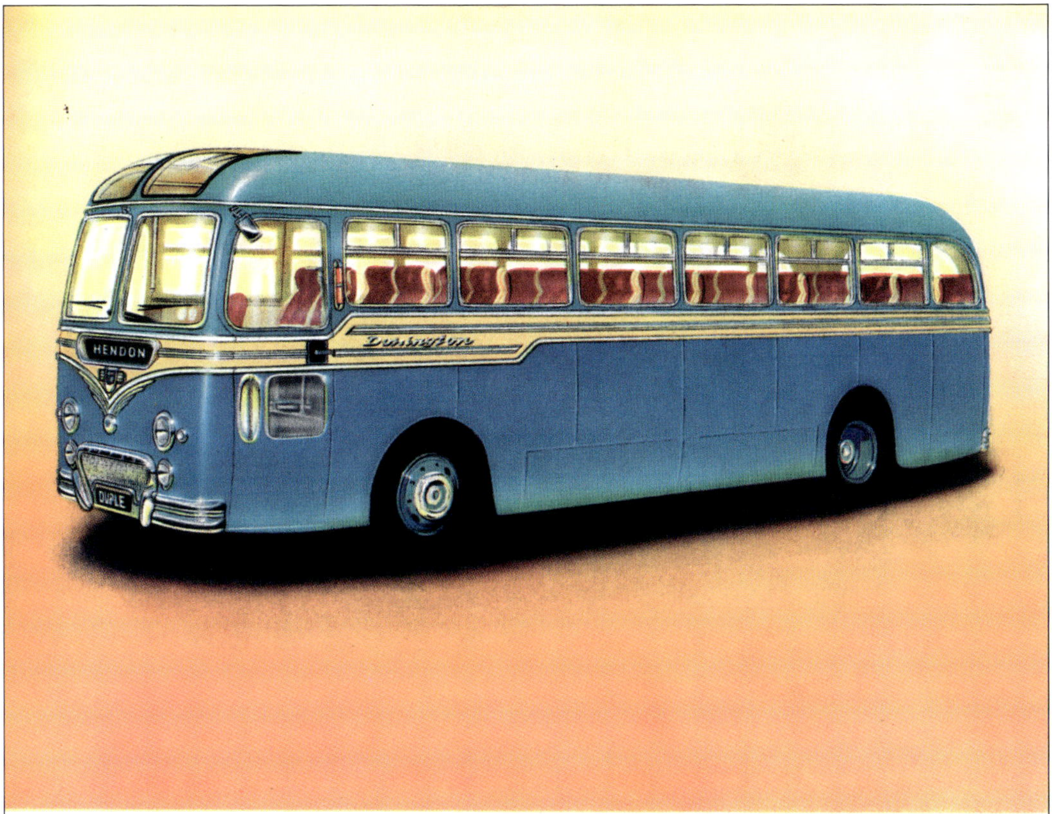

The Duple DONINGTON

43 passenger metal-framed luxury coach

THIS is the 1957 Duple 43-passenger lightweight metal-framed luxury coach with stressed interior skin. It includes special features in construction and finish that mark it as a leader in its class. Mounted on A.E.C. Reliance or Leyland Tiger Cub chassis and constructed to the full luxury specification, including Rockite/Formica finishers, it is available with alternative moulding arrangements. Toughened safety glass is fitted throughout and bumpers are of super-purity aluminium with anodized finish. There is a large capacity baggage locker and three metal-framed Perspex roof lights, the front and rear with 3-way adjustment — the centre panel fixed. Built at Duple Motor Bodies (Midland) Ltd.

DUPLE MOTOR BODIES LTD., THE HYDE, HENDON, LONDON, N.W.9. Tel.: COLindale 6412

Conventional double-deckers

Aberdonians unfairly have a reputation for being tight-fisted, which may explain the headline 'When economy is the order of the day'. Featured in this 1957 AEC advert, coinciding with a Scottish Motor Show, is an Aberdeen Corporation 1955 Regent V with a Crossley body, unusually with a Gardner rather than AEC engine. A South Wales Reliance/Park Royal helps to maintain the UK balance.

In this 1957 advert, Guy is making the case for buying its Arab IV model by suggesting a saving of £166 per vehicle per annum – an uninspiring figure today, but a point worth making more than 60 years ago, when £166 was the equivalent of £4,000 today. Northern General has opted for the exposed radiator version of the chassis on these 1956 Park Royal-bodied buses.

Willowbrook used the tilt-test to advertise its double-deck bodies – here, a 1956 Walsall Daimler CVG6 on the tilt-test is joined by a 1956 East Yorkshire AEC Regent V, Derby 1953 Sunbeam F4 trolleybus, Walsall 1953 Sunbeam S7, 1956 Stratford Blue Leyland Titan PD2 and a West Bromwich 1956 Daimler CVG6 – showing no fear or favour to any chassis manufacturer!

Opposite: Leyland continued to use facts and figures in its advertising. In this 1957 advert, it uses a map, centred on Leyland, Lancashire, showing towns and cities where the local municipal operators have placed orders for more than 1,000 Leyland double-deckers. The coverage is impressive, with a cluster of more than 20 within relatively easy reach of the Leyland plant, including substantial fleets like Liverpool and Manchester. A 1956 Manchester Titan PD2 with Metro-Cammell body is used to illustrate the point.

Lower and longer

Several chassis builders recognised that passengers were not happy with the awkward lowbridge layout that kept the overall height of double-deckers down with an awkward side upstairs gangway and four-across seating; seeing the successful Lodekka model developed by Bristol and ECW for state-owned fleets, they conceived equivalent models, none of which came anywhere close to achieving the same success. Dennis tried a different approach and obtained a licence to build the Lodekka for customers unable to buy from Bristol. This 1958 advert for the Loline shows an East Lancs-bodied example for Aldershot & District, which became its main customer.

The Loline was developed in a forward-entrance version, as seen here for Walsall Corporation in this 1960 Willowbrook advert, but without great success in spite of the superlatives in the advert.

With the legal length of double-deckers increased to 30ft (9.1m) in 1956, MCW was quick to produce a lengthened version of its lightweight Orion body, seen here on a Potteries example, doctored to show the MCW logo in place of the PMT one. In 74-seat form, MCW was still claiming a body weight of a little over two tons (2,032kg) in a bus weighing just over 7½ tons (7,742kg). This six-bay body style was quickly replaced by a less fussy five-bay version.

Opposite: The Bridgemaster was designed by Crossley for the ACV Group, as seen in this slightly glamourised 1956 advert.

The 'BRIDGEMASTER'

The low height 'Bridgemaster' is a new conception in double-deck bus design.

The 'Bridgemaster' has an unladen height of only 13 ft. $5\frac{5}{8}$ in.— achieved by integral construction and the use of offset transmission with a specially designed rear axle to give low floor height. It has, too, central gangways in both saloons for speedier passenger flow. Independent front suspension and coil spring suspension provide maximum comfort.

Every design feature of the 'Bridgemaster'—Britain's new leading double decker—can be inspected on Stand 57.

STAND 57
COMMERCIAL MOTOR
TRANSPORT EXHIBITION
EARLS COURT, LONDON

A.C.V. SALES LIMITED
49 BERKELEY SQUARE, LONDON, W.1

P.R.V. GROUP BODY SALES DIVISION
PARK ROYAL VEHICLES LIMITED
Abbey Road, Park Royal, London, N.W.10

AN A.C.V. GROUP PRODUCT

CV.318

London's Routemaster

London Transport's Routemaster turned out to be the ultimate half-cab front-engined double-deck type. Developed over a number of years, and tested in prototype form from 1954, by the end of the 1950s it was ready to go into production as a joint AEC/Park Royal product. With only the 1954 prototype available for illustration, Park Royal announced in 1957 that it had been awarded the first production order, which was for 850 buses.

AEC also announced the order in a 1957 trade press advert, featuring the same image as the Park Royal advert, but rendered strangely, making use of the red second colour, which gives it a ghost-like appearance.

Another 1957 Park Royal advert for the Routemaster order, this time with a mocked-up colour illustration showing the slightly bulbous revised front end that resulted from the decision to move the radiator from under the engine to the front.

1956–60: Double-Deck Developments

In its 1958 form, the Routemaster was closely based on the prototypes, with a more attractive front-end treatment. This AEC advert appeared in 1960 when the Routemaster was in full production. In 1958, few of the most optimistic observers would imagine that Routemasters would still be in revenue-earning service in London 60 years later, but this view of a 1964 Stagecoach example in service in 2017 confirms their longevity, admittedly on a heritage route.

New ideas

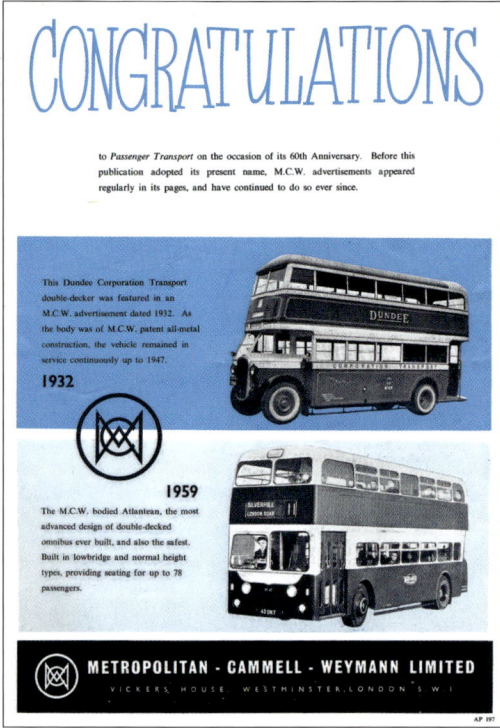

MCW offered its congratulations to the trade magazine *Passenger Transport* on the publication's 60th anniversary in 1959, showing a 1932 Dundee Corporation Thornycroft Daring and one of the four 1958 pre-production Leyland Atlanteans, the semi-lowheight version for Maidstone & District.

The 1956 advert features the prototype of Leyland's brand-new Atlantean, which at this stage was an integral bus completed by MCW, although the copy does not actually mention its collaborators. Although the copy suggests this was 'The bus with *your* ideas... but built by *us*', there were many reservations among operators who examined it, leading to a rethink and the reappearance of the Atlantean as a separate chassis two years later.

Mulliners of Birmingham was mainly a builder of car bodies that, in the 1950s and 1960s, also built bus bodies. This rather exaggerated advert showing a futuristic-looking body style that was actually built on Guy Warrior chassis, was published in 1958, the last year Mulliners built bus and coach bodies.

Opposite: Early in 1957, MCW was advertising the Atlantean as a Leyland chassis with MCW bodywork, still using an image of the 1956 prototype as the model might appear later in 1958, before operators were able to see completed pre-production examples. The advert refers to an order for 20 for Wallasey Corporation, which received one of the 1958 buses.

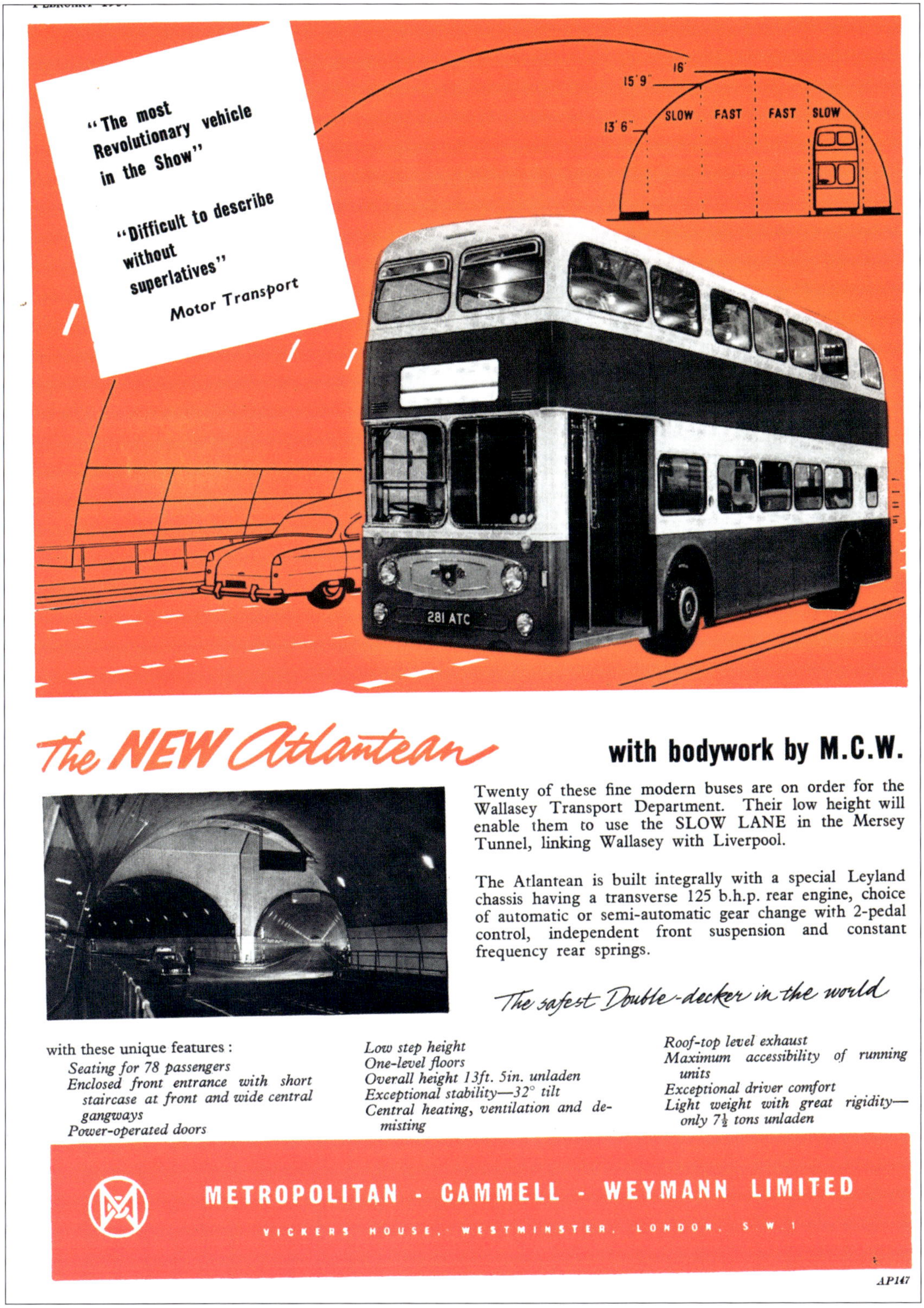

The NEW Atlantean
with bodywork by M.C.W.

"The most Revolutionary vehicle in the Show"

"Difficult to describe without superlatives"

— Motor Transport

Twenty of these fine modern buses are on order for the Wallasey Transport Department. Their low height will enable them to use the SLOW LANE in the Mersey Tunnel, linking Wallasey with Liverpool.

The Atlantean is built integrally with a special Leyland chassis having a transverse 125 b.h.p. rear engine, choice of automatic or semi-automatic gear change with 2-pedal control, independent front suspension and constant frequency rear springs.

The safest Double-decker in the world

with these unique features :
- Seating for 78 passengers
- Enclosed front entrance with short staircase at front and wide central gangways
- Power-operated doors
- Low step height
- One-level floors
- Overall height 13ft. 5in. unladen
- Exceptional stability—32° tilt
- Central heating, ventilation and de-misting
- Roof-top level exhaust
- Maximum accessibility of running units
- Exceptional driver comfort
- Light weight with great rigidity—only 7½ tons unladen

 METROPOLITAN - CAMMELL - WEYMANN LIMITED
VICKERS HOUSE, WESTMINSTER, LONDON, S.W.1

AP147

Chapter 5

1961–65 Single-Deck Developments

The early 1960s are remembered for the spread of longer, often rear-engined bus and coach chassis, and the beginning of a period of great change in the British bus and coach manufacturing industry that would continue for decades, until there were a mere handful of UK builders still standing, and competitors from mainland Europe and well beyond were firmly established in British fleets.

The upheaval had started in 1960 when Daimler was sold to Jaguar, to be joined by Guy a year later. Then, in 1962, came the shock of AEC selling out to Leyland and the creation of the Leyland Motor Corporation in 1963, followed by Leyland acquiring a stake in Bristol and ECW that brought their products back on the open market after 17 years.

Bristol and ECW had developed significant models during the years when they built only for state-owned fleets, in particular the lowheight Lodekka and the rear-engined RE. No Lodekkas were sold on the open market, but there were plenty of customers for the single-deck Bristol RE when it became

AEC used this dramatic view of a Harrington Cavalier-bodied Reliance from the Yelloway fleet to proclaim its superiority. Certainly, the long-lived Reliance proved to be a popular chassis for bus and coach work in Britain and throughout the world.

By 1962, AEC was part of the growing Leyland group, and the Reliance continued to compete with Leyland's equivalent Leopard model. In this 1964 advert, an anonymous Leopard bus with a BET-style body is featured along with a 1927 Leyland Lion, oddly, and a Duple Continental coach that might just be a doctored photo of a Reliance.

1961–65: Single-Deck Developments

generally available. This chassis had been successfully introduced in 1962, and was followed by rear-engined single-deck models from AEC, Daimler and Leyland, though it is fair to say that none of these were held in the same high esteem as Bristol's RE.

Daimler had wasted no time in designing the double-deck Fleetline chassis, a rival to Leyland's Atlantean, and cleverly specified a drop-centre rear axle that allowed it to carry bodies built to a lower height than contemporary Atlanteans, important for operators with low bridges on important routes. Although Leyland would later offer similar variations on its Atlantean, it is best remembered as a full-height urban bus.

When buses and coaches up to 36ft (11m) long were legalised in 1961, there were many bus operators who regarded a full-length 53-seat single-decker as a viable alternative to double-deckers, particularly if standing passengers, sometimes up to 24 of them, were taken into consideration.

Not every operator rushed to buy buses and coaches of the new maximum length, but many took the opportunity to specify vehicles to lengths that sat somewhere between 30ft (9.1m) and 36ft (11m). This allowed slightly longer double-deckers, offering more internal space, and when 33ft (10m) double-deckers followed, a seating capacity of up to 83 passengers was possible.

Coaches also got longer, often increasing potential seating capacity from 41 to 49. The AEC Reliance and Leyland Leopard became the main chassis choices for heavier coaches to the new length, although Bedford and Ford, supplying lighter chassis into both bus and coach fleets, were looking at building to new length. Bedford got in first with its innovative VAL model, a three-axle twin-steer chassis that spread the axle load more evenly. Ford, nipping at Bedford's heels for lighter-weight chassis orders, produced its two-axle R226 in 1965.

Duple still dominated the coach body market, but Harrington and Plaxtons were both working hard to attract business with distinctive new ranges.

In many ways, the early 1960s can be seen as years of relative calm before the major restructuring of both the manufacturing and operating industries towards the end of the decade, which would have a significant impact on the shape of the bus industry and, sadly for the publishers of the trade monthlies, on the amount of income they could attract to stay in circulation.

MCW was keeping its options open in this 1961 advert, showing a forward-entrance Halifax Leyland Titan PD3 and a Sheffield front-entrance Leyland Atlantean.

Ford was giving Bedford a good run for its money with the Thames 36 chassis, later the Ford R226, a two-axle competitor for Bedford's three-axle VAL. Success at the annual Blackpool and Brighton coach rallies was always an opportunity to advertise, as seen here in 1965.

1960s double-deck variety

After the disappointing reception for its advanced 1959 Wulfrunian model, Guy returned to what it did best – the tried and tested Arab, in this case the Mark V version introduced in 1962. The chassis was lower built to make passenger access easier, and it remained available until 1971, by which time Guy and Daimler, together under Jaguar since 1961, had passed to British Leyland along with what had become British Motor Holdings, combining Jaguar with the troubled British Motor Corporation.

There was a move to forward-entrance bodies on front-engined chassis from the late 1950s, and in 1961 MCW featured a Halifax Leyland Titan PD2 as an example of what could be done.

AEC replaced its integral Bridgemaster lowheight double-decker with the Renown chassis in 1962, but it may have been too late on the scene, as Leyland and Daimler had already introduced their rear-engined models, and buses like the Renown were sometimes regarded as old-fashioned. This 1963 advert shows a Park Royal-bodied Renown for the South Wales fleet.

Opposite: More Leyland figures in this 1964 advert, which highlights the 76.29 per cent of municipalities that used Leylands, adding in small print that 40.5 per cent of all municipally owned buses were Leylands, and there were 7,175 Leylands in municipal service, mostly, the illustration could imply, front-engined types, but balanced by the image of a Liverpool Atlantean.

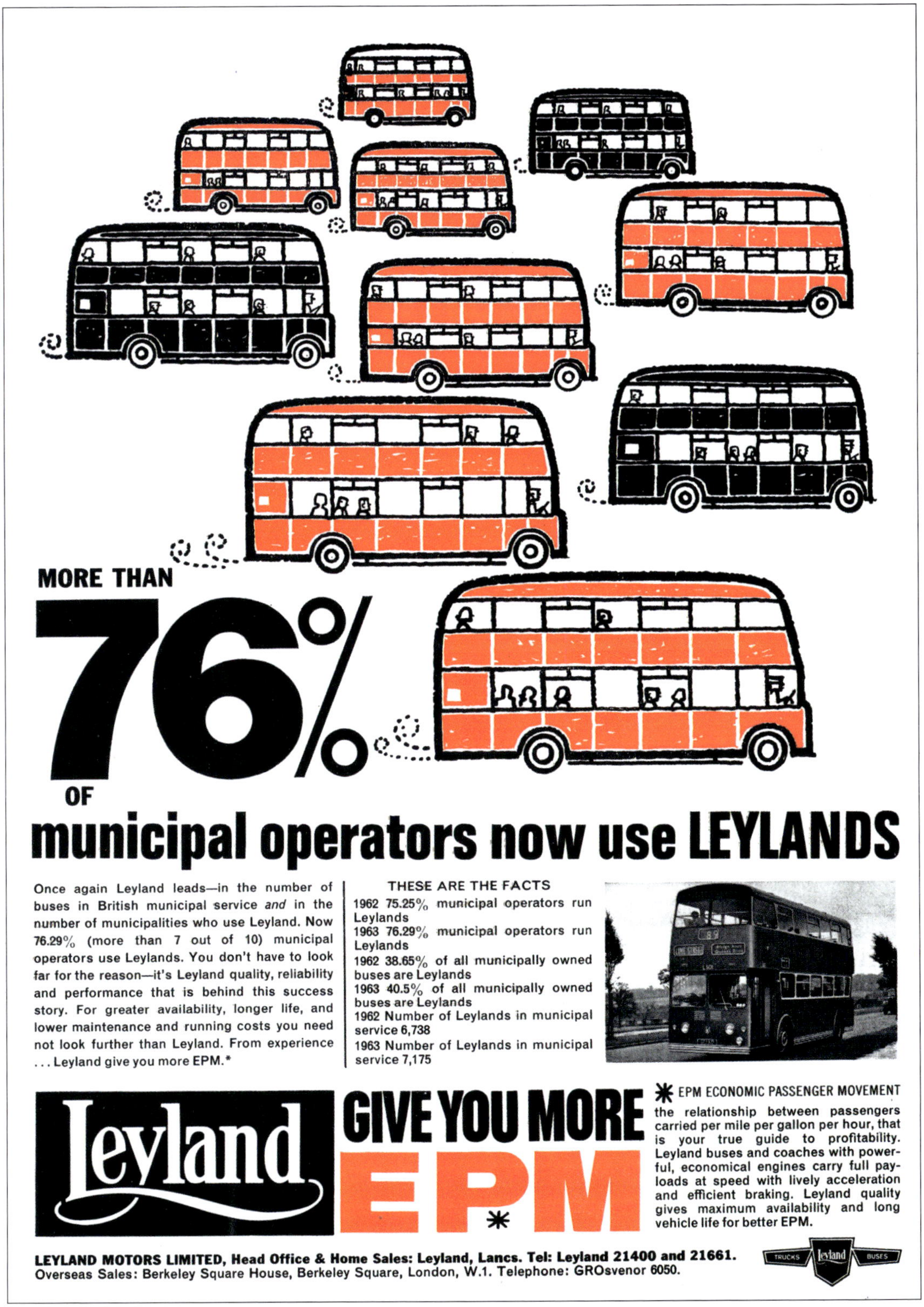

1961–65: Single-Deck Developments

MORE THAN 76% OF municipal operators now use LEYLANDS

Once again Leyland leads—in the number of buses in British municipal service *and* in the number of municipalities who use Leyland. Now 76.29% (more than 7 out of 10) municipal operators use Leylands. You don't have to look far for the reason—it's Leyland quality, reliability and performance that is behind this success story. For greater availability, longer life, and lower maintenance and running costs you need not look further than Leyland. From experience ... Leyland give you more EPM.*

THESE ARE THE FACTS
1962 75.25% municipal operators run Leylands
1963 76.29% municipal operators run Leylands
1962 38.65% of all municipally owned buses are Leylands
1963 40.5% of all municipally owned buses are Leylands
1962 Number of Leylands in municipal service 6,738
1963 Number of Leylands in municipal service 7,175

Leyland GIVE YOU MORE EPM

*✱ EPM ECONOMIC PASSENGER MOVEMENT the relationship between passengers carried per mile per gallon per hour, that is your true guide to profitability. Leyland buses and coaches with powerful, economical engines carry full payloads at speed with lively acceleration and efficient braking. Leyland quality gives maximum availability and long vehicle life for better EPM.

LEYLAND MOTORS LIMITED, Head Office & Home Sales: Leyland, Lancs. Tel: Leyland 21400 and 21661.
Overseas Sales: Berkeley Square House, Berkeley Square, London, W.1. Telephone: GROsvenor 6050.

MCW used a series of innovative adverts using in-service photos of its products, like this Bournemouth Corporation Leyland Atlantean with a body style that owed more than a little to contemporary Alexander designs.

Liverpool Corporation never operated blue MCW-bodied Leyland Atlanteans, but the vagaries of using the designated second colour led to this 1963 advert using blue rather than Liverpool's normal green. The MCW bodies for Liverpool broke away from the rounded look of early bodies on rear-engined double-deckers and led the way for more inspired designs from other builders. Leyland still could not resist the temptation to throw in some figures – four years and 150 million miles in this case.

Walter Alexander (Coachbuilders) was growing fast in the 1960s, but only advertised in the trade press at the time of London and Glasgow motor shows. This 1963 advert features two of its most popular body designs – the A type double-deck body, seen here on a Glasgow Leyland Atlantean, and the adaptable Y type single-deck body; the 1961 prototype on AEC Reliance chassis for Scottish Omnibuses is shown here. Alexander moved its coachworks to Falkirk in 1958.

Opposite: Daimler promoted its new Fleetline chassis as a bus that would be equally at home on inter-city work and on the city streets. Prototype MCW-bodied Fleetline 7000 HP features in this 1961 advert.

ONE BUS — TWO JOBS

INTER-CITY with **78 seats** FLAT FLOORS & CENTRAL GANGWAY **CITY**

- ELIMINATES THE LOW BRIDGE PROBLEM
- DRIVER CONTROLLED DOORS
- OUTSTANDING ECONOMY
- LOW MAINTENANCE COSTS (GARDNER) AND AUTO-BRAKE ADJUSTERS
- REAR ENGINE

TRANSPORT VEHICLES (DAIMLER) LTD., G.P.O. BOX No. 29 COVENTRY TEL: COVENTRY 27626 (15 lines)
Full technical information on request

New single-deck developments

Daimler's Roadliner was the least successful of the breed of rear-engined single-deck chassis introduced in the early 1960s. One problem was the range of engines offered, unfamiliar Cummins, British Leyland and Perkins units. In this 1967 advert featuring a Plaxton-bodied bus, there is no mention of the original Cummins unit.

Marshall of Cambridge rose to prominence as a bodybuilder in the 1960s and 1970s, with bodies like this version of the BET Group standard design on Leyland Leopard chassis in this striking 1965 advert showing a Southdown example.

Strachans bodies were available for many years, and by the time this advert appeared in 1964 the business was based in Hamble, in Hampshire. It features unusual bodies built on Bedford's twin-steer VAL chassis for North Western, allowing a route to pass under a very low canal bridge.

Opposite: Leyland's rear-engined single-deck models were the Panther and the shorter and less powerful Panther Cub, illustrated in this 1965 advert with a Park Royal-bodied two-door example majoring on its manoeuvrability. The Panther sold relatively well in home and export markets, more than the sometimes troublesome Panther Cub.

1961–65: Single-Deck Developments

Leyland

FOR MAXIMUM PASSENGER CAPACITY WITH GREATER MANOEUVRABILITY

THE LEYLAND PANTHER CUB

The 33ft. Panther Cub, built for greater manoeuvrability in crowded towns provides smooth, silent, vibrationless travel. This is because the Leyland 0.400 diesel engine is mounted underfloor, rear of the back axle to carry engine noise away from the passengers. The 43-seater bus illustrated here was bodied by Park Royal Ltd. and the unencumbered Panther chassis, designed for easy low front entry, gives the widest possible scope to body designers.

LEYLAND MOTORS LTD. Head Office and Home Sales: Leyland, Lancs. Telephone: Leyland 21400 and 21661
☐ ☐ ☐ ☐ Overseas Sales: Berkeley Square House, Berkeley Square, London, W.1. Telephone: GROsvenor 6050

Dodge re-entered the British bus market in 1962 with the lightweight front-engined S306 chassis, intended to compete with Bedford and Commer models, but few were built. This image represents the 1962 Weymann-bodied 42-seat prototype.

Major builders, best known for their service bus bodies, sometimes dipped a toe in the luxury coach market, often unsuccessfully. Park Royal tried with two very different designs, both named Royalist, in the 1950s and 1960s, while arch-rivals MCW also tried without much success in the 1960s with this, the not unattractive Metropolitan, which could be built on Bedford or Ford chassis. This 1967 advert emphasises the £3,995 purchase price (equivalent to over £77,000 in 2022 terms). Manufacturers were usually very coy about actual prices. The Metropolitan name would resurface in 1973 for a Scania-based MCW double-deck model.

Mercedes-Benz made a first tentative foray into the British market with this 1962 advert for its 0-321 model and although it led to no orders, it was an early indication of the increasing role than European bus and coach builders would play in the British market over the next 60 years.

One of a fleet of Duple-Daimler 45-seater Roadliners for Edmonton, Alberta.

Duple win big Canadian bus order
against world competition

DUPLE GROUP SALES LTD. Edgware Road, The Hyde, London, N.W.9. Tel: Colindale 6412
LONDON, LOUGHBOROUGH AND BLACKPOOL

An early success for Daimler's Roadliner was an order from Edmonton in Canada for Duple-bodied examples. This artist's impression in a 1965 Duple advert exaggerates the length of these buses – compare it with a photo of the real thing from a 1967 Daimler advert.

Duple dominates

Bedford's three-axle twin-steer VAL model in 1962 made it possible for lightweight coaches to be 36ft (11m) long, and Duple complemented it with the 52-seat Vega Major body, here in typically Duple exaggerated form in a 1963 advert.

Left: This 1965 line-up of Duple's range demonstrates a certain family resemblance at the front ends, although most look as they have been 'updated' since the photo was taken. The coach types are, from the right: the Vega Major on Bedford VAL; Mariner on Ford R226; Commander on AEC Reliance; Continental on AEC Reliance; Bella Venture on Bedford VAM; Empress on Ford R192; Viscount on Bedford VAM; Vista 25 on Bedford VAS; and Duple (Midland) body on Bedford J2.

Opposite: Another Duple 1963 model was the Dragonfly, built by Duple (Northern) at the former Burlingham coachworks at Blackpool. It was a full-length 36ft (11m) body for AEC or Leyland heavyweight chassis, oddly with a centre entrance. In spite of its exaggerated appearance in this 1962 advert, few were built.

The Cavalier and the Leopard

Operators enthusiastically invested in 36ft (11m)-long coaches in the 1960s, and manufacturers were keen to reflect this in their advertising. This Harrington advert featuring a Leroy Tours AEC Reliance with Cavalier 36 body in Innsbruck appeared in 1962.

More than three years later, the same photo of the same coach was used in this 1965 AEC advert.

Well, if this isn't the limit...

...at the moment, 36 ft. *is* the new legal limit for P.S.V.s. And, as usual, Leyland have anticipated the increase—with the Long Leopard bus and coach models. A natural successor to the 30ft. Leopard, which is already many operators' first choice on long distance routes, this new model is designed to give even more profit per passenger mile. And if this *isn't* the limit, and a new one is fixed in the future—Leyland will be ready for that too. They always are.

36 FT LONG LEOPARD

up-to-the-minute—
built to the limit

LEYLAND MOTORS LTD., Leyland, Lancs.
Sales Division: Berkeley Square House, Berkeley Square, London, W.1.   Tel: GROsvenor 6050

Leyland enjoyed great success with the 36ft (11m) version of its underfloor-engined Leopard, as shown with a Plaxton Embassy body in this 1962 advert. Leyland had responded quickly with chassis to this new legal length and suggests that 'if this *isn't* the limit, and a new one is fixed in the future – Leyland will be ready for that too'. And when longer coaches were legalised in 1967, Leyland was ready.

Coaching in the 1960s

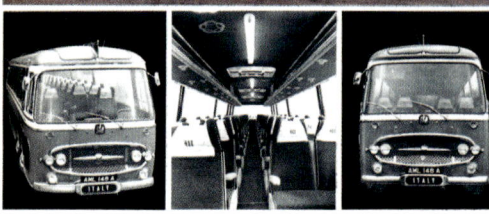

Western SMT was an early customer for Leyland's Leopard, buying 20 with Alexander 30-seat bodies for its overnight Glasgow–London services, and the 1961 advert tells you, in typical Leyland fashion, that they average just under 17mpg on this long run, while each vehicle logs 3,000 miles weekly.

MCW's first coach body for the longer chassis was the Castilian, seen here looking much longer than its 36ft (11m) in an artist's impression for this 1962 advert. It was built on Leyland Leopard chassis for Southdown.

Plaxton was emerging as a credible rival to the mighty Duple empire, particularly following the introduction of its Panorama, which led to wider use of longer side windows in coaches and, to a lesser degree in single-deck and double-deck buses.

The coach shown in this 1963 advert was built on Bedford VAL chassis for Whitefriars Coaches of Wembley, sporting an early year-suffix registration.

Opposite: Plaxton was obviously proud of this substantial order for 35 Panorama bodies on Leyland Leopard chassis for Ribble, featured here in a 1964 advert.

Innovative adverts

By the 1960s, some advertisers, encouraged no doubt by their advertising agencies, produced adverts that were visually very different to the sometimes staid and formulaic efforts of the 1940s and 1950s. MCW produced a series of eye-catching black-and-white photographic adverts; this 1964 example shows an MCW-bodied AEC Regent V of Bradford Corporation at speed.

Ford was starting to rival Bedford for the lucrative lightweight coach business but was still omitting the Ford name and promoting its products under the Thames PSV name in this interesting 1963 advert, showing a chassis and passengers but no body. The Ford name would eventually be emphasised.

A very subtle 1965 advert by glassmaker Triplex – what looks like a Duple-bodied coach rendered purely in black-and-white with a small Triplex mark on a window, where these marks are to be found, though in a somewhat smaller size.

Opposite: Plaxton had abandoned the 's' of the Plaxtons name-style by the time this daring advert appeared in 1965. It is clearly a coach and, to potential customers, clearly a Plaxton coach without adding anything much more in text.

Chapter 6
1966–70
Moving to Standardisation

Everything, it seemed, was up for grabs in the late 1960s. The process of mergers and acquisitions in the manufacturing industry that had started in the early 1960s now moved into a higher gear. In 1966, Jaguar, which owned Daimler and Guy on the bus side, merged with the British Motor Corporation to create British Motor Holdings (BMH), and two years later Leyland and BMH merged to create the unwieldy giant that was British Leyland (BL), bringing together Britain's ailing car industry with the major names in the bus and truck business. So, AEC, Albion, Bristol, Daimler, ECW, Guy, Leyland, Park Royal and Roe were now together under common ownership, and clearly something had to be sacrificed to ensure future viability – but in the government's eyes, it was the BL car division that needed most attention and investment, to the detriment of the development of the bus and coach range. Beyond 1970, this led to a series of discontinued models, plant closures and what nobody could possibly have imagined at the time, the acquisition of Leyland by the Swedish giant Volvo.

Daimler worked hard to promote its rear-engined Roadliner chassis as a basis for bus or coach bodywork but without much success, in spite of a changing selection of engine options that did not appear to appeal to British operators. This 1965 advert features a Duple Commander-bodied coach.

Bus and coach overall lengths increased in the 1960s, and manufacturers rushed out longer versions of existing models. Leyland promoted its 33ft (10m)-long Atlantean in this 1966 advert, highlighting the extra passengers that buses of this length could carry.

Added to this was the creation of the first Passenger Transport Executives (PTEs) in 1969–70, which absorbed 20 previous municipally owned operations, which, between them, operated over 6,400 buses, and led to centralised buying of new highly standardised buses to replace their mixed inheritance, and its knock-on effect on existing manufacturers.

One positive development that was welcomed by manufacturers and operators alike was the New Bus Grant scheme, which, from 1968, subsidised the cost of new buses to a specification that allowed driver-only operation, to the tune of 25 per cent of vehicle cost, rising to 50 per cent before being phased out by 1984. This led to a rush to buy Bus Grant vehicles, which helped the industry, at least in the short term.

Unaffected by much of this was the coaching sector, the operators of all sizes that provided private hires, day and extended tours and express services. While the large groups, Tilling, BET and Scottish Bus, were involved in all of these activities, so were independent operators ranging from substantial businesses to family firms with perhaps just one coach. So, as the number of advertisers chasing bus business continued to decline, there was still scope for builders of new coaches.

But sadly, not enough. The final edition of the leading monthly, *Bus & Coach*, was published in February 1970. The final edition ran to just 44 pages, which included only 13 pages of paid advertising – a far cry from the heady days of the 1950s, when there could be 40 pages of editorial and over 100 pages of adverts.

London Transport's unhappy experiences with the rear-engined AEC Swift family chassis led to the production of this 1978 booklet aimed at prospective buyers. The cover shows a barely seven-year-old Swift with Park Royal two-door body.

Daimler and standardisation

Daimler concentrated on standardisation in its late 1960s advertising. The colour photo version of Daimler's standardisation adverts shows examples of Fleetline models with the same operator, Rochdale Corporation. The double-decker has an MCW body in this 1969 advert, and the single-decker was bodied by Willowbrook.

The 1968 advert featuring blue single-deck and double-deck Fleetlines concentres on the advantages of the many common features they share, using Leeds Roe-bodied and Grimsby-Cleethorpes Willowbrook-bodied examples.

With 25 per cent government grants available for new buses that met certain criteria – notably their suitability for driver-only operation – Daimler directed potential customers towards a publication of its own in this 1969 advert.

Opposite: Another 1968 Daimler advert takes this a stage further with representations of single-deck and double-deck Fleetlines of varying shapes, sizes and door configurations. In contrast to the popular double-deck version, the single-deck Fleetline was not a big seller.

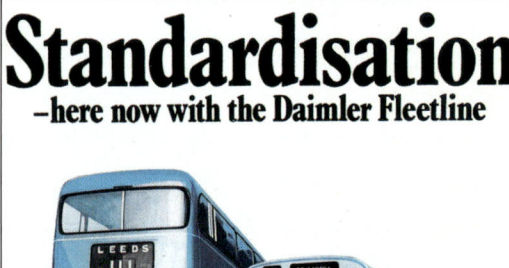

Standardisation
–here now with the Daimler Fleetline

left: 30 ft. Fleetline double decker with front entrance.
below: 33 ft. Fleetline single decker with front entrance.

left: 30 ft. Fleetline double decker with central exit.
below: 33 ft. Fleetline single decker with central exit.

left: 33 ft. Fleetline double decker with front entrance.
below: 36 ft. Fleetline single decker with front entrance.

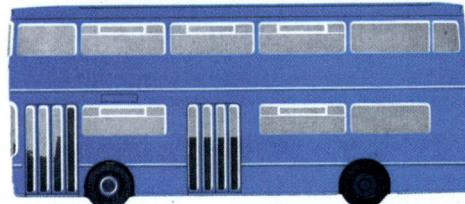

left: 33 ft. Fleetline double decker with central exit.
below: 36 ft. Fleetline single decker with central exit.

The advantages of Standardisation are obvious. Its introduction is another matter and, initially, could be very costly. **But not for Daimler Fleetline operators!**

The already well proven features of the Fleetline double decker have now been extended into single deck versions and offer the operator a complete range of vehicles for all types of operation, on one basic design of chassis with standardised running units. Double deck chassis are available with 30ft. and 33ft. overall lengths and single deckers with 33ft. and 36ft. overall lengths.

Standardised running units include Gardner 6LX engines with 6LW and 6LXB alternatives; the Daimler epicyclic gearbox with right angle drive, and the dropped-centre drive axle.

And not only the main units are standard. Virtually all auxiliary components are common to every Fleetline chassis, which will please your maintenance and stores staffs.

If you already operate Fleetlines, we invite you to consider the other variants available. If not, the introduction of Fleetlines could be a short step to Standardisation. Either way, let us send you full technical specifications.

DAIMLER TRANSPORT VEHICLES LTD., COVENTRY, ENGLAND.
Tel: Coventry 27626 (15 lines)

Coach market competition

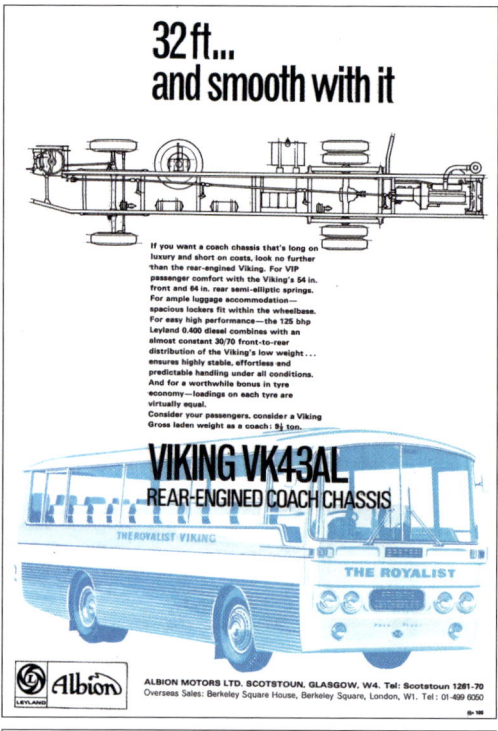

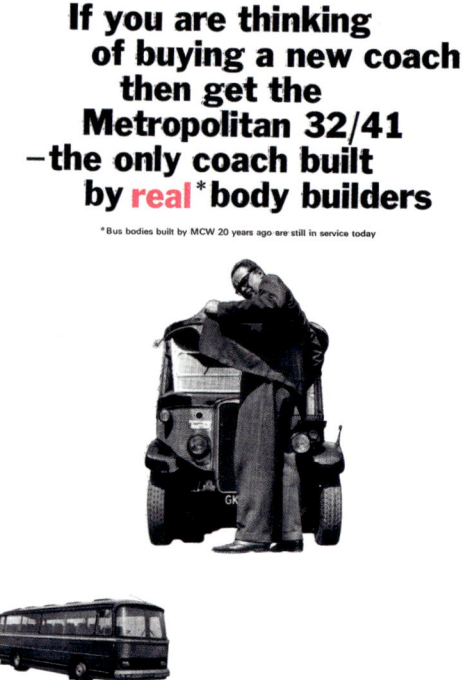

Albion's rear-engined Viking was primarily bought for service bus duties, but, as part of the Leyland Group, Park Royal offered its Royalist body on this chassis, but few were built. This is a 1967 advert.

Bristol's LH was an adaptable underfloor-engined chassis and was popular with bus and coach companies. This 1969 advert extols the virtues of both roles.

Another interesting advert from MCW, this time still promoting its Metropolitan coach in 1967, although the 1931 Green Line Duple-bodied AEC Regal is given rather more prominence than the not-unattractive Metropolitan. Duple and Plaxton might have had problems with MCW's claim that it was 'the only coach built by real bodybuilders', a claim supported by the slightly irrelevant fact that 'Bus bodies built by MCW 20 years ago are still in service today', although 1947 buses were thin on the ground by 1967.

Opposite: Duple coaches were still selling well on medium-weight chassis like the Viceroy-bodied Bedford VAM in this 1969 advert, as well as on heavyweight chassis.

Plaxton prominence

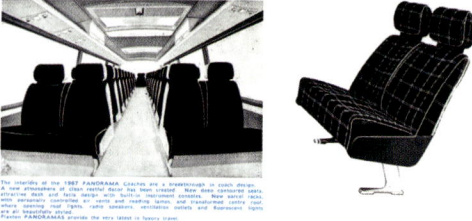

The Plaxtons (now with the 's' revived) Panorama Elite body introduced curved side windows 'for extra passenger comfort'. This is a Wallace Arnold example on Leyland Leopard chassis, in a 1969 advert.

The AEC Reliance was still selling well to coach operators in 1966 – it would still be available until 1979. This 1966 advert shows a Sheffield United Tours example with Plaxton Panorama body.

The Panorama helped to change Plaxton's fortunes with wide side windows and slim window pillars. This anonymous version appeared in a 1966 advert.

Opposite: Another subtle Plaxton advert, a 1967 example showing – just – a Panorama body on Bedford VAM chassis. By this time, Plaxton had become a strong challenger for the luxury coach body market.

1966–70: Moving to Standardisation

Plaxton

Plaxtons (Scarborough) Ltd., Castle Works, Seamer Road, Scarborough. Tel: 63311

Double-deck choices

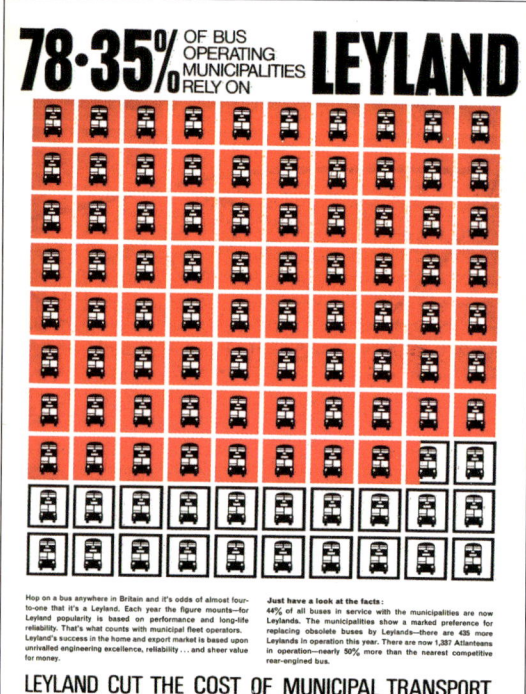

Above: This advert for the Leyland Atlantean, featuring a Southampton example with Blackburn-built East Lancs body, was the cover advert on the very last issue of *Bus & Coach*. 'At Leyland we care about passengers', reads the copy, but the photo shows passengers boarding from the roadway. Leyland, as usual, included a statistic highlighting the fact that 'over 72% of all municipalities run Leylands in their fleets'.

Opposite: A Daimler advert published to coincide with the 1969 Scottish Motor Show features a 33ft (10m) long Fleetline with Alexander bodywork supplied to Western SMT, with a blue second colour in the advert rather than Western's actual red. The copy mentions that 'the Fleetline is designed to qualify for the 25% grant proposed in the recent Transport Bill'. The small British Leyland logo appears beside the familiar Daimler one.

Park Royal was still advertising its bodywork on the AEC Routemaster in 1967, this time featuring the forward entrance version supplied for BEA in 1966–67 and operated by London Transport.

An unusual 1966 advert by MCW, showing recent double-deck deliveries to the Plymouth, Birmingham and Manchester municipal fleets, against the backdrop at Elmdon of Leyland-MCW Olympics from the vast orders bound for Cuba – and the MCW car park.

Leyland was still using statistics in this 1966 advert boasting that 78.35 per cent of bus-operating municipalities relied on its products. The representation of a bus appears to be based on STF 90, the 1954 Saro-bodied Leyland FEDD rear-engined prototype.

New looks and a new chassis

Left: Park Royal regularly booked the front pages of the trade magazines its full-colour adverts. The 1966 advert features a Sheffield Leyland Atlantean pictured against a backdrop of central Sheffield, including the railway station and the Park Hill flats complex.

Leyland featured its newly available 33ft (10m)-long Atlantean in this 1968 advert, an option that was taken up by several operators looking for higher-capacity buses. The advert shows a new Manchester Corporation Leyland Atlantean with the ground-breaking Mancunian body style.

Opposite: Bristol was able to advertise double-deckers after some 20 years, when its products were again available on the open market. Its previous model, the Lodekka, had been available only to state-owned fleets, and the 1968 advert refers to it – 'we don't have to tell you how successful that was – and is!'. The VRT joined the Atlantean and Fleetline as part of Leyland's double-deck range.

Bristol's new V.R.T.
Another winner from the Lodekka stable

Here it is – the first quantity production double-decker chassis from Bristol since the Lodekka (we don't have to tell you how successful that was – and is!)
The new VRT with Vertical Rear Transverse engine has so many outstanding features, including its very competitive price.

Choice of Engines
Gardner 6 LX or 6 LXB; Leyland O.680.

Simple Maintenance
The Bristol VRT chassis has only eight grease points. Engine and gearbox unit enclosed by moulded G.R.P. structure permits easy access to all parts of the power unit and gearbox.

Clean Comfortable Cab
Floor, offside and instrument facia are moulded from G.R.P., with controls placed to reduce driver fatigue.

Stainless Steel Brake Piping
Drop Axle yet Removable Differential
Optimum Performance
Road speeds of 63 m.p.h. and gradient ability of 1 in 4 can be achieved.

Excellent Choice of Optional Alternatives
The Bristol VRT chassis having the engine and gearbox unit mounted transversely at the extreme rear of the chassis caters for double or single deck body work.
Please write for more information.

BRISTOL COMMERCIAL VEHICLES LTD
BRISLINGTON BRISTOL BS4 3LD
TELEPHONE BRISTOL 77613

Single-deck variety

Many bus operators chose medium-weight chassis for service work on less demanding routes. Albion developed the rear-engined Viking VK43AL with Scottish Bus Group orders in mind, as older front-engined single-deckers came up for replacement. This 1968 advert features an Alexander Y type bodied example for Alexander Midland.

For more intensive service, operators usually chose larger-engined chassis like the Leyland's rear-engined Panther, here with Marshall's impressive Camair body for Northern General. The list of other customers is mildly misleading, as the Gateshead, Sunderland and Tyneside companies all belonged to the Northern General group.

Ford was making its presence felt in the lighter-weight bus and coach market, directly competing with Bedford for orders from operators of all sizes. In this 1967 advert, a Strachans-bodied R192 delivery to Birmingham City Transport is featured.

Opposite: Bedford's VAM model sold well in coach and bus form, and this 1968 advert shows a recent delivery to The Eden with a Plaxton Derwent body – although the bodybuilder does not get a mention.

1966–70: Moving to Standardisation

The Bedford VAM brings real versatility to PSV operation. It's designed to!

With Bedford's own 466 cu. in. diesel, the VAM front entrance 41/45 seater takes the toughest *touring, staging or municipal* duties in its stride. It's designed to.
Like all Bedford vehicles, it's precision-engineered for day-in, day-out reliability.
The set back front axle allows for up to 80 in. overhang and there is plenty of room for front entrance doors and steps. Wheelbase 193 in.
The low first cost of the VAM (£1,732-10) and low replacement costs make this rugged vehicle a most economical investment.
Bedford put power under PSV bonnets and profit into PSV operation. For you.

Bedford
Bedford vehicles are designed to do the job.

The rear-engined single-deck chassis introduced in the mid-1960s enjoyed varying degrees of success. The Swift was AEC's offering, dubbed the Merlin in big-engine form for substantial deliveries to London Transport, which favoured larger single-deckers for a time. This 1966 advert shows a London Merlin with Strachans bodywork used on the innovative Red Arrow service.

Above: The future of Leyland's range of rear-engined single-deck chassis would be decided in the 1970s, following the introduction of the integral Leyland National model, a joint venture between Leyland and the National Bus Company. The first indication of this future came in this dramatic 1970 advert.

Opposite: The first, and to many the best, of the rear-engined single-deck chassis was the Bristol RE, available to all customers from 1965 and on the lists until 1982, but latterly only for 'export chassis', which was a means of ensuring continued deliveries to Northern Ireland! This is a 1969 advert.

The rear-engined Leyland Panther shared some of its design features with the AEC Swift, now the companies were together under Leyland. This is a 1965 Panther with Roe body for Kingston upon Hull Corporation, in a 1966 advert where the yellow second colour really has not worked.

Other books you might like:

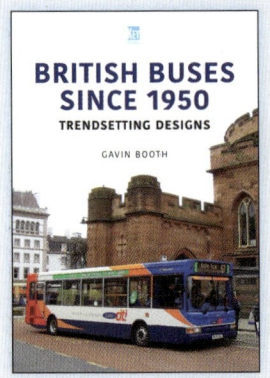

Britain's Buses Series, Vol. 10

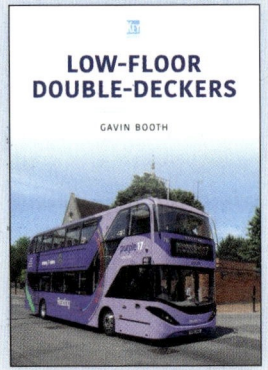

Britain's Buses Series, Vol. 9

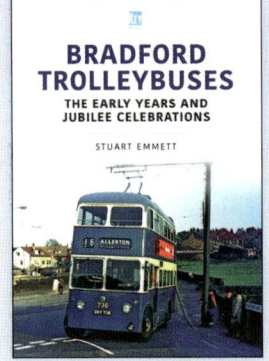

Britain's Buses Series, Vol. 11

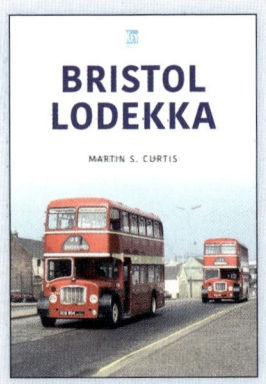

Britain's Buses Series, Vol. 3

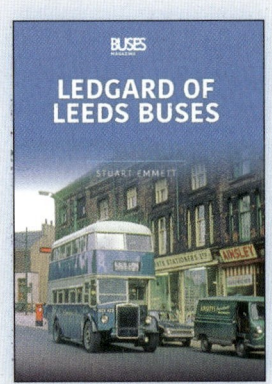

Britain's Buses Series, Vol. 1

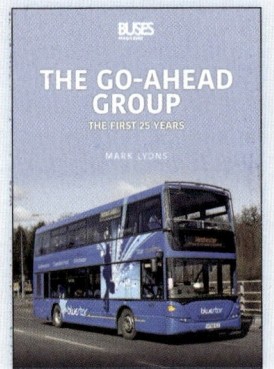

Britain's Buses Series, Vol. 5

For our full range of titles please visit:
shop.keypublishing.com/books

VIP Book Club

Sign up today and receive
TWO FREE E-BOOKS

Be the first to find out about our forthcoming book releases and receive exclusive offers.

Register now at keypublishing.com/vip-book-club

Our VIP Book Club is a 100% spam-free zone, and we will never share your email with anyone else. You can read our full privacy policy at: privacy.keypublishing.com